The 'Cornish Riviera Express'

A VIEW FROM THE PAST

STEPHEN AUSTIN

Ian Allan

PUBLISHING

Cover: The afternoon sun glitters and flashes off every wave in Mount's Bay, dazzling and delighting passengers who, a few hours earlier, could see no further than the house across the street. Cases are heaved off the racks as they make ready to alight into the bright light and clear air of the Cornish Riviera. The driver who has brought the 'Cornish Riviera Limited' down through Cornwall brakes the train to a stop in Penzance station. A drift of smoke comes from the engine's fire, made up so as to keep her simmering for a couple of hours before the return trip to Plymouth with the 'Postal'. 'Enchantment fills the scene.' (Nicholas Mitchell) *Painted for this volume by George F. Heiron*

Title page: The new train for the summer 1956 season was complemented by a new headboard painted cream with brown lettering and with a Cornish shield on top. In this view from 1956 or 1957 the train is double-headed up Dainton Bank. The leading engine cannot be identified as the BR numberplate is covered by the train number, while the rear engine is enveloped in steam escaping from its glands and snifting valves. *J. Scott-Morgan collection*

First published 2000

ISBN 0 7110 2723 4

Published by Ian Allan Publishing

an imprint of Ian Allan Publishing Ltd, Terminal House, Shepperton, Surrey TW17 8AS. Printed by Ian Allan Printing Ltd, Riverdene Business Park, Hersham, Surrey KT12 4RG.

Below: The only part of the route that was never doubled was the Royal Albert Bridge. This view is from the up 'Limited' crossing into Devon on a day in 1960. The lettering on the bridge arch was ordered not by Brunel but by the Cornwall Railway directors. No doubt the man who put that walkway on the same face had an unimpeachable reason for arranging it to obscure the memorial. *P. Q. Treloar*

Contents

Above: A publicity line-up at Old Oak Common Depot to advertise the 'King' class. No 4004 *Morning Star* and No 5010 *Restormel Castle* are upstaged by No 6000 *King George V*. This was taken just after the latter returned from America in December 1927 and shows the modified front axle springs, American bell and B&O medals. *LPC*

Prologue

As we enter the 21st century, the counties of Devon and Cornwall are becoming increasingly obsessed with tourism as a source of income — an 'industry' as it is now called — indeed, a way of life. This originated with the Great Western Railway's creation of the Cornish Riviera as a place, an institution and above all as a train: the greatest of all the holiday trains that promised sea air and green hills to the city-bound. Even more impressive was the creation of a new public image of the railway company, which hitherto had been widely distrusted in the West Country. It is to the credit of the GWR personnel that they built up the new tourism business in Devon and Cornwall, helped the farmers and fishers, made a little profit for their shareholders and established a place for themselves in popular affection. This little album is a celebration of that achievement.

This is not a complete history of the 'Cornish Riviera Express', but rather a view of its origin and development over the first half of the 20th century.

Right: A notable combination on the down 'Limited' on Friday 17 December 1954. The train engine is No 6000 *King George V*, and from Newton Abbot the pilot is No 1000 *County of Middlesex*, proudly bearing the prototype GWR double chimney. They are working up speed on the level section out to Aller Junction. The train is made up to 13 coaches, all Hawksworth stock except for the 1923 kitchen and diner, sixth and seventh coaches by the signal, and the ninth, which looks like a 1938 60ft.
D. S. Fish

CORNISH RIVIERA EXPRESS: A View From the Past

To assemble this view from the past, I have enjoyed the privilege of delving into the library of Ian Allan Ltd, which includes views collected before World War 2 by their predecessors, the Locomotive Publishing Co (LPC), Locomotive & General Railway Photographs (LGRP) and Real Photographs Co (RP). Some photographs came from the late lamented Great Western Railway itself, some from photographers who are no longer with us and some from those who are still making their work available for us all to enjoy. To them all we owe our gratitude. I would also like to thank the Railway Studies Library of Newton Abbot, David Fish, Derek Reynolds, Ian Canavan, the late Kenneth Leech, Dick Riley, Fred Elton and John Blyth for help and material.

It would be presumptuous to highlight as superior any of the wealth of books published on every aspect of the Great Western Railway, so I will just say that the following have been particularly useful:

Railway World magazine
The GWR in West Cornwall , A. Bennett
Atlas of the GWR , R. Cooke
Great Western Coaches from 1890, Michael Harris
GWR Engine Sheds (London Division), C. Hawkins and G. Reeve
Railway World Special — Cornish Riviera, Chris Leigh
History of the GWR Vol. II, E. T. McDermot
GW Express Passenger Locomotives, Martin Smith
The Cornwall Railway, R. J. Woodfin

1. The Story

When the 20th century began, a respected scientist said that all the important discoveries had now been made and all that was left was to refine a few details. So far as applied science is concerned, our experience since then has been confirmatory. The technologies we have used over the subsequent century were in essentials brought into being by an astonishing surge of research and development which occupied, roughly, the two decades from 1890 to 1910. The motor car, the aeroplane, radio, the telephone, recorded music, automatic data processing, the electronic valve, the steam turbine, the generation and distribution of electric power, the urban tube railway, the oil engine, control of radioactivity — all were products of this era. If an engineer of the time were translated forward to the end of the 20th century, he would be impressed by the spread of technology but would see little that was basically unfamiliar to him.

This surge of creativity was quite unprecedented. (The only thing that came near it was the similar 20-year period a century earlier that saw the steam locomotive change from a curiosity to a practical transport tool.) The intoxication of progress, led by scientists and engineers, spilled over into other sectors of society. This was the time when fiction writers turned out stories of detectives beating crime by science, of men travelling through time, even of space-flight. In those heady days, anything seemed possible.

At this time the Great Western Railway experienced a renaissance. It had been in a state of stagnation and retrenchment for many years following the economic crisis of the 1860s, a stasis whose end was symbolised by the deaths of the broad gauge and of Sir Daniel Gooch.

The rebirth was marked by the appointment of N. J. Burlinson as Superintendent of the Line in 1888. He represented a new management style: improving the company's performance not by reductions but by expansion and better services. The first practical expression of this policy appeared in June 1890 in the form of a new West of England express, named the 'Cornishman'. It left Paddington at 10.15am and reached Bristol in two and a half hours (the first time this speed had been scheduled since 1848), Exeter in 4hr 5min, Plymouth in 5hr 35min and Penzance in 8hr 42min. The up service left Penzance at 11.15am and took 2hr 55min to Plymouth, 4hr 15min to Exeter, 6hr 3min to Bristol and 8hr 35min to Paddington. It conveyed a coach to and from Newquay, which soon grew to form a separate train during the peak season, running a few minutes in front of the 'Cornishman' proper. The timing of this introduction was not coincidental; June 1890 was when the London & South Western Railway (LSWR) began running over its own route to Plymouth.

Burlinson retired in April 1894 and his successor, T. I. Allen, continued his policy, first with an overnight London-Penzance service, then with a long-overdue measure: he bought out the refreshment room franchises, particularly the notorious one at Swindon. Hitherto all trains had to pause there for at least 10 minutes. Its elimination from 1 October 1895 cleared the way for not only faster trains but the prospect of beating the record, currently held by the Great

Above left: In the post-Edwardian summer, about 1912, the second part of the 'Cornish Riviera Limited', which left Paddington at 10.35am, is seen from the platform at Hanwell & Elthorne station. The engine is 'Star' No 4030 *King Harold*, built in 1909 and recently fitted with an improved boiler. The first of nine coaches is a 40ft luggage van, followed by a 70ft brake composite. *Bucknall Collection*

Left: The July 1935 'Centenary' train, now the 'Cornish Riviera Express', running through Sonning Cutting on an up journey. The special coaches, distinguished by inset doors, have been augmented by one of the older type dating from 1929. The engine is 'King' No 6012 *King Edward VI*, built in April 1928. *M. W. Earley*

Left: The postwar 'Cornish Riviera' passing Twyford on Sunday 19 August 1951. A variety of coaches, some (including the first) the latest type with flat sides, hauled by 'King' No 6025 *King Henry III*, presenting a patriotic, if garish, spectacle: the engine bright blue and the coaches red and cream.
M. W. Earley

Below: A typical express of the 1890s, picking up water from Goring trough on its way from Bristol to London. The troughs were actually at Basildon (43½ miles from Paddington); the bridge in the background carries the road from the village to the church. The engine is No 16 *Brunel*, which started life as a broad gauge 2-4-0 in 1886. She was rebuilt as a 4-4-0 in 1894 and is seen here as running about the turn of century with one of the first of Churchward's domeless boilers, leaving little of the original machine except the name.
Bucknall Collection

Eastern Railway (GER), for running without a stop. From 20 July 1896 the Newquay portion of the 'Cornishman' ran nonstop between Paddington and Exeter, 193 miles, in 3¾hr. This was by a handsome margin the longest run made by any public service train in the world. At first it was done in summer only, extended to all the year round by the up train in 1899 and by the down train in 1902.

The vital factor in this nonstop working was the locomotive water supply, as the largest GWR tender carried only 3,500gal, so replenishment on the move was essential. In preparation for nonstop running to Bristol, water troughs were installed at Basildon in the Thames Valley, and a set at Fox's Wood near Keynsham enabled trains to run past Bristol as well. However, in 1902 another set of troughs was laid at Creech, near Taunton, for Allen had it in mind to reach even further.

In 1902 King Edward VII and Queen Alexandra visited Dartmouth to dedicate the foundation stone of the Royal Naval College

and went on to a reception in Plymouth. On Friday 7 March the Royal Train left Paddington at 10.30am and ran nonstop to Kingswear in 4hr 23min. This was a record of 228 miles, but it stood only until the following Monday. The returning Royal Special started from Millbay Docks at 11.30am. At Millbay Junction the two tank engines which had lifted it from the dock line were removed, and the couplings, left slack to negotiate the curves, were closed up. It left there at 11.40 and arrived at Paddington at 4.24pm — 246¼ miles nonstop in 4hr 44min. The locomotive on both these historic runs was No 3374 *Baden Powell* of the 'Atbara' class, carrying the name *Britannia* for the occasion.

These runs attracted tremendous public interest. The *Daily Telegraph* put a reporter on board and his piece the following day, under the headline 'Making A Record: A Royal Progress', said that they were 'likely to have a far-reaching effect, having regard to the eagerness of the owners of large ocean-going vessels calling at

Above: During the races from Plymouth in 1904-6 the GW went to the extreme of slipping the Bristol portion of the Ocean Mail special in order to avoid stopping it. This view, which was widely circulated at the time, shows the slip taking place as the train approaches Bedminster station 'at 69mph'. The unique slip van No 837, with No 863 trailing, drops back while the front part, two 68ft vans, continues on its nonstop Plymouth-Paddington run. *Great Western Railway*

Plymouth to take advantage of the smallest saving of time on the railway journey'. As the train passed through Exeter station it slowed to pick up the London newspapers and a gun salute was fired from the town. Large crowds were noted in Plymouth, Newton Abbot, Dawlish, Taunton and Bridgwater; in Bristol there were 'children in white pinafores thronging the refuse-heaps of the manufacturing quarter' and at Swindon the entire 12,000 workforce turned out to watch. The travellers were themselves equally enthusiastic and, 'it was

generally known that His Majesty had made himself familiar with every detail of the working of his train'.

To readers brought up in the over-regulated late 20th century, using a Royal Train for such an experiment seems rash, but the worst that could happen was the train being stopped. Railwaymen are a wilful lot, and even if they were ordered not to obstruct a train there was no guarantee that they would not do so by some exploitation of the rules. However, the rules for working a Royal Train included stopping goods trains, locking and guarding level crossings, and so on, so that the vital clear road could be enforced. Besides, at that time corporate spirit was high on the GWR and when it came to carrying royalty the staff could be depended upon to 'pull out all the stops'. It was thus quite logical that a royal journey should be used for the next distance trial. It took place on Tuesday 14 July 1903 and the train was the leading portion of the 'Cornishman'; besides the

Prince and Princess of Wales in the Royal Saloon, there were some ordinary passengers on board the five coaches. It left Paddington at 11.40am and ran nonstop to Plymouth North Road, 245¾ miles.

The amazing feature of it was that, although due in at 3.10pm, it appeared in North Road station at 2.33½, having done the trip in 3hr 53½min at an average speed of 63.4mph. After Milepost 200 passed in exactly three hours, the *Daily Telegraph's* correspondent heard a GWR officer say, 'I never saw anything like it — we shall have to do a lot of retiming.' 'Ah!' retorted another official, 'Today we are masters of the signalmen; they are not ours!' That astonishing achievement, not only by the crew on the engine, No 3433 *City of Bath*, but also by the maligned signalmen and by the fitters and engineers responsible for the equipment, was one which will never be surpassed.

These operations could be dismissed as non-commercial stunts, but the managers had a serious objective, which was to make long-distance travel more attractive to the passenger. In demanding faster and more comfortable trains, they had the enthusiastic support of the engineering staff at Swindon. Engineers love to spend their employers' money to prove that they can make things bigger, louder and faster; with this encouragement from head office, Swindon became a forcing-house of engineering talent whose young enthusiasts would come to dominate the 20th century British railways. Among their number were John Robinson, William Stanier, Richard Maunsell, James Holden, Surrey Warner and Charles Collett.

The railway was soon transformed. Main lines were doubled and quadrupled, the Brunel track was replaced by cross-sleepered track, the 'Stert & Westbury' and 'Castle Cary & Langport' lines to the west, and the 'Ashendon & Aynho' line to the north, were built, new designs for station, goods shed and

THE CORNISH RIVIERA.

Jane and all

THE LIZARD LIGHT—EVENING.
(From a drawing by C. G. Harper.)

Within easy reach of London, the Midlands and the North.

Issued by the
GREAT WESTERN RAILWAY COMPANY,
PADDINGTON STATION,
LONDON, W.

FRANK POTTER,
General Manager.

June, 1914. [COPYRIGHT]

Left: The book by E. M. Bradley which introduced 'The Cornish Riviera' to the British public. This is a 1914, fourth edition copy, printed by Harrison & Sons of London. *Author's collection*

locomotive depot buildings were produced and applied on a huge scale, and radically new locomotive and rolling stock designs appeared. But unfortunately for the shareholders, engineers tend to go around asking, not 'Is it profitable?' or even 'Does it give a better service?' but 'Is it technically clever?' Matters soon reached a state in which developments were being driven by the engineers, much as they had been in the 1840s.

The Locomotive, Carriage & Wagon Superintendent, William Dean, retired in May 1902 and was succeeded by his assistant, George Jackson Churchward, who although Swindon-bred had a new style. Unlike his austere, alarming predecessor, he was jovial and hearty. He dressed casually in tweeds, appearing as if he had looked in after a day's fishing, which was indeed his favourite hobby. He was a good leader, popular with the men; his engine crews were proud of the engines he gave them, and for British workmen to admire

Above: No book on the 'Limited' could omit the historic photograph, taken by the company photographer, of the inaugural down train passing Acton Yard on the morning of 1 July 1904. The French 4-4-2 No 102 *La France* hauls a brake third, third, first, 'dreadnought' restaurant, second and brake third. Another photographer is standing on the right with what was, for those days, a small portable camera. *Great Western Railway*

any new tool imposed on them from head office is practically unknown. He enjoyed making statements calculated to shock people — for instance, when in 1904 the question arose of faster schedules to counter the London & South Western Railway's new Plymouth ocean liner expresses, he said that as far as he was concerned they could all go out and break their bloody necks; and he said that, for all the passengers cared, GWR coaches could be coated on the outside with tar so long as the seats were comfortable.

Top: New equipment in 1905, in the form of a 'City' class engine (it could be No 3433 *City of Bath*) and, seventh coach, one of the first 'dreadnoughts', which were restaurant cars. The last coach is in an all-over brown livery which was then being tried as an alternative to the familiar chocolate and ivory. This express is heading west past Acton Yard. The modern signals with their 5ft arms contrast with the 1876-type siding signal on the right. *LGRP*

Above: An express embodying the era of transition. The 'City' class engine has a new taper boiler with wider chimney and feed clack valves on top. The train is an up express of two portions, perhaps Penzance and Falmouth or Newquay. The 12 coaches include Churchward 'toplights' at the rear, Dean 'clerestories' at the front and two older luggage vans. The date of this view is probably about 1908. *LPC*

Left: The first express 4-6-0, No 100 *William Dean*, with the second of the series of experimental boilers, on the down 'Cornishman' in May 1904, coming out of Kennaway Tunnel. One of the new 'dreadnought' restaurant cars stands out (literally) from the 'clerestories'. The notice 'ORDINARY SPEED RESUMED' refers to a speed limit through Coryton Tunnel, immediately behind the camera, where engineers had started widening work. *LGRP*

Below: An up secondary express from Exeter passing Twyford on the relief line in August 1912. Five 'clerestories', four 'dreadnoughts', another 'clerestory' and two six-wheelers which, at the tail end, must have given their occupants a mighty rough ride. The engine is No 3716 *City of London*, built in 1903 but already demoted from top-rank duties. In the distance are the signalbox and, beyond the main road bridge, the station. *H. Gordon Tidey*

Right: The west side of Paddington station in about 1912. Among the formally attired travellers are some casual gentlemen with button-down collars and soft hats, and fashionably modern ladies in jackets and plain hats. The clock, then only a couple of years old, shows 10.30, so if that is the 'Limited' it is going to be late starting. That may explain why the crew of the saddle tank engine which brought in the empty stock are looking towards the barrier to see if the station master is going to hasten it. The near coach, obviously new and attached behind the Weymouth slip coach, may be conveying a special party, causing the delay. *Ian Allan Library*

Centre right: At Penzance, also in around 1912, the driver of 'Bulldog' No 3428 *River Plym*, built in 1903 and recently fitted with a superheated boiler, poses for the camera; on the left is one of the ubiquitous saddle tanks. Above the 'Bulldog' is the railing erected in 1852 to discourage the populace from throwing missiles at the new station roof. *IAL*

Below right: An express leaving Paddington in about 1908, passing under Westbourne Road Bridge and between Westbourne Road signalbox and Platform A, which was then open to the public. No 3713 *City of Chester* hauls a set of new 'toplight' coaches. Engineers are inspecting and repainting the bridge and have slung access platforms beneath it. The siding by the train was used for fire-cleaning before the Ranelagh Bridge engine yard was built. *LPC*

However, he was profligate with the company's money; a Swindon locomotive cost 50% more than a similar Crewe product. He countered this with petty, futile economies and did carry out his carriage paint threat by replacing the famous chocolate and ivory livery with a drab brown. And he was absolutely besotted with all things American. He imported American designs for coaches, big open saloons which the British public did not like, and for locomotives of a type which, although now familiar to anyone who has seen a Wild West movie, were very exotic in the days before ordinary folk had seen anything of America. He admired American 'hustle' and contempt for tradition, and he was responsible for the destruction of the last two broad gauge locomotives, preserved by his predecessor.

This let's-throw-away-the-baggage-of-tradition attitude is infectious and brought about the ocean liner race of 1904. The LSWR built a new terminal at Stonehouse for receiving small numbers of VIP passengers off transatlantic ships, and marked its opening on 23 April by whisking the first consignment up to London in 4hr 3min: a good ¾ hr inside the current 'Cornishman' schedule. The GWR response was the famous run of 9 May, in which a train of mails left Millbay at 9.23am and stopped in Paddington at 1.10pm. The 3hr 47min included 4min standing at Bristol for changing the engine. This was just a sideshow, of course. The main event of 1904 was that the GWR invented the Cornish Riviera.

In view of the fact that South Cornwall is still (in AD2000) using the title, it is a pity that its exact origin has not been better recorded by history. It is probably fair to say that it had no single source. Travel writers had for many years been eulogising Cornwall's climate as comparable with that of the Mediterranean coast, and such reputable guides as Black's and Kelly's emphasised the same. In 1876, the year when the GWR took over the South Devon, Cornwall and West Cornwall Railways, unifying the entire route, the town of Penzance issued its

Left: In 1913 at Westbourne Bridge, Platform A has been shortened to make room for another track into the parcels station and new connections are being laid into Ranelagh Bridge engine sidings. The train, probably the 'Limited', is hauled by new 'Star' class 4-6-0 No 4042 *Prince Albert*. *LPC*

Above right: 'Saint' class 4-6-0 No 2983 *Red Gauntlet*, built in 1905, hauls an up express through Sonning Cutting in 1913. The train is a mixture of 'toplight', clerestory and 'dreadnought' stock. The disparity in outline of the various types of GW coaches made it clear that they were of different ages. Other companies' trains were just as polytypic, but did not show it so much. *Bucknall Collection*

Centre right: Riviera resort: Penzance in about 1930, viewed from Lescudjack Hill. Low down in front of the harbour is the station roof and to the left is Albert Quay with a line of wagons on it. Across the harbour (occupied mainly by pleasure craft) is the Ross Swing Bridge and above it is the tower of St Mary's Church, a welcome landmark to generations of seafarers. *Author's collection*

Below right: Riviera resort: Porthminster Beach, St Ives, in about 1923. It is a sunny day and a few people are paddling but all are fully clothed. On a ledge above the beach can be seen the goods shed and main building of the station, which extends right round the bay. *Author's collection*

first tourist guide book. In 1904 came the book *The Cornish Riviera*, written by E. M. Bradley of the Publicity Department at Paddington, which, with its subtitle *Our National Health & Pleasure Resort — How to go there and What to see there*, set out straight away to establish 'The claims of the Cornish Littoral to a share of the patronage once bestowed almost exclusively on its foreign rivals.'

The launch of the book coincided with a new express from London to Penzance with a through coach for Falmouth. For regular nonstop working to Plymouth a further water supply was deemed necessary, so troughs were laid at Exminster and were in use when a trial run was made to the new schedule on 30 June 1904, using the stock which would form the inaugural up train. The locomotive was again *City of Bath*. The new service began on Friday 1 July. Scheduled time to Plymouth was 4hr 27min down and 4hr 25min up. It was, again, the world distance record for a service train, although it should be noted that *Baden Powell's* 1902 record was broken on 19 and 22 July 1903 by the London & North Western Railway's *Commonwealth* and *Charles H. Mason*, which took a special from Euston to Carlisle and back, 299 miles nonstop each way. Paddington departure was at 10.10am (the 'Cornishman' left at 10.40) and arrival at Penzance was 5.10pm, with calls at Plymouth, Truro, Gwinear Road and St Erth. The up train left Penzance at 10am, called at St Erth, Gwinear Road, Truro, Devonport and Plymouth and reached Paddington at 5pm. The inaugural down train in 1904 was hauled by the French-built locomotive No 102 *La France* as far as Plymouth and by 'Bulldog' No 3418 *Paddington* from Plymouth to Penzance. The up train, always given less attention, was worked by anonymous 'City' class engines.

It did not run in the 1904 and 1905 winters, but on resuming on 1 July 1906 it stayed all the year round. (During those winters the 3pm Paddington-Falmouth and 7.10am Falmouth-Paddington held the world record by running nonstop to and from Exeter.) It was already so popular that sometimes the down train had to stop at Newton Abbot to attach an assisting engine for the steep gradients onwards to Plymouth, thus nullifying the nonstop gimmick.

Some way of limiting the numbers of passengers asking to use it had to be found, so it became the first train in which seats had to be reserved in advance.

At this time the periodical *The Railway Magazine* suggested the train should have a name and, after toying with *The Three Towns Flyer*, invited its readers to submit ideas. The GWR General Manager, Sir James Inglis, judged the entries and chose the title *The Riviera Express*, submitted by F. Hyman and J. Shelley. However, because of its connection with the book, it was already being known as the *Cornish Riviera Express* and that was the name adopted in the 1906 timetable. The railwaymen had already given it their own nickname. Because of the schedule, the traffic staff were, in theory, forbidden to add extra coaches to the formation, and in the Service Timetable it was annotated 'Limited Load'. It thus became known as the 'Limited'. In a short while this name spread among railway enthusiasts and then to the general public to such a degree that eventually even the management acknowledged its use — so we will use it in these pages to help capture the ambience.

As mentioned above, the introduction of the 'Limited' was timed to outshine the LSWR's Stonehouse ocean liner terminal. The new coaches for it were not ready — they came on in 1905 — but from then on it was regarded as the

Above right: In the mid-1920s the chocolate and ivory livery returned, although the engine here has not yet received the decorative brass beading on windows and wheel splashers, which disappeared during the war. She is 'Star' No 4065 *Evesham Abbey*, built in December 1922 and destined to work the last steam-hauled 'Bristolian' on 12 June 1959 and to continue in service until 1964. The train is made up of 70ft 'toplights' except for the fourth coach, which is a 'dreadnought'. It is a down express about to pass Twyford station. *H. Gordon Tidey*

Right: In this express, hauled by a 'Star', pulling away from Penzance in the 1920s, the first coach is a 'dreadnought', the second a 'toplight' and the rest are the new steel-panelled stock introduced from 1923. On the far left is the edge of the massive rock filling which replaced the original viaduct at this point. *P. Ransome-Wallis*

company's premier train and received the latest and best in locomotives and coaches. When these notes were being written in 1999, the coaches used on the Cornish expresses reached their 20th anniversary of continuous service. Such a situation was unknown in the heyday of the 'Limited', whose passengers rode in stock that was new or had seen only one overhaul, until World War 2 stopped progress and resulted in the use of vehicles up to 10 years old.

When the new route from Reading to Taunton via Westbury was completed the 'Limited' was one of the first trains switched to it, on 21 July 1906 down and 23 July up. The distance to Plymouth was now 226 miles, still the world record, and for nonstop purposes troughs were provided at Aldermaston and Fairwood, at about the same mileages as Basildon and Fox's Wood. The booked time was reduced to 4hr 10min each way. Departure from Paddington was put back to 10.30am but departure from Penzance remained at 10am, and about then a quaint little ceremony developed. At that time each day a time signal was sent down the telegraph system to all stations on the railway. At Penzance the station master stood by the open door of the telegraph office and, when he heard the instrument register the 'ten' signal he blew a horn. The guard waiting by his van door waved his flag and the driver, similarly waiting, started his engine. The time from Penzance to London was 6hr 45min; from London to Penzance was 6hr 40min, pared to 6hr 30min by 1914.

Also in 1906 the power of the new 4-6-0 locomotives enabled the 'Limited' load to be increased, so extra coaches were added for Torquay, Minehead, Ilfracombe and Weymouth. To avoid stopping, slip coaches were used, detached at Exeter, Taunton and Westbury, so that the train left Paddington with three slip portions at the rear, another record in its way. The only slip which ran in summer was that for Weymouth; on peak days the 'Limited' took a full load through to Cornwall and extra trains served the other resorts. Slipping was done only on the down run, the service up from those places being markedly inferior. For this reason, from September 1906 the winter up 'Limited' called at Exeter. It is possible that there were even thoughts of cutting out stops in Cornwall,

for in 1908 the Engineers proposed water troughs adjoining Lostwithiel station, on one of the few level stretches in the county, but they were not built. In 1914 through coaches were added for Newquay and St Ives, but slipping was not required as the train stopped at Par and St Erth.

Connecting services were an important part of the operation. Stops at St Erth, Gwinear Road, Truro and Par made connections with the branches, and by 1914 the GWR owned a fleet of road motor coaches. These plied from Penzance to St Just, Land's End and Marazion; Helston to Porthleven and The Lizard; Redruth to Portreath, Falmouth and Carharrack; St Austell to St Dennis, St Blazey Gate and Bugle, and Saltash to Callington. The company also subsidised independent firms, and after the Grouping the GWR and SR (Southern Railway) between them kept a 50% holding in the Devon General, Western National and several smaller omnibus companies.

By 1914 the newspaper *The Cornishman* noted with some misgiving that, 'the ever-increasing influx of well-to-do visitors... is rapidly transforming some of the Cornish fishing ports into holiday resorts,' and that prices were rising. The GWR had clearly succeeded in establishing the new industry — tourism — and, whether beneficially or not, had redirected economic trends in the region.

Wartime conditions did not affect the 'Limited' overmuch until 1 January 1917, when the Government, in control of all the railways, drastically reduced and slowed services. In effect, the 'Limited' ceased to exist as an express. Stops were put in at Westbury, Taunton, Exeter, Newton Abbot and all stations through Cornwall and slipping ceased. It took 7¾ hr to reach Penzance and 8hr to return. The title and the status returned for the first summer after the war, on 7 July 1919. Nonstop running with the Taunton and Exeter slips resumed, the Westbury slip came back the next year and from 3 October 1921 the schedule was exactly as it had been in 1914. But another shake-up was on the way.

The Government did not relinquish control of the railways until 15 August 1921 and immediately followed that with a Railways Act which forced them to form the 'Groups'. On the GWR Felix Pole took over as General Manager

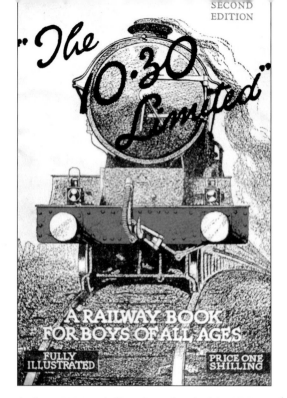

A RAILWAY BOOK
FOR BOYS OF ALL AGES

BY W. G. CHAPMAN

PUBLISHED IN 1923 BY
THE GREAT WESTERN RAILWAY
[FELIX J. C. POLE, GENERAL MANAGER]
PADDINGTON STATION, LONDON

in June 1921 and Churchward retired in 1922, to be succeeded by his Assistant, C. B. Collett.

The period that followed is best known for an outpouring of publicity. *Holiday Haunts in England and Wales*, first issued in 1906, had by the 1920s grown to a 500-page catalogue. The 'books for boys of all ages' by W. G. Chapman appeared in the summer of 1923 and the first title was, as you would expect, *The 10.30 Limited.* This use of the colloquialism in print shows how popular culture had changed as a consequence of the war; this was the Jazz Age

Above: The cover and title page of *The 10.30 Limited,* the first of the 'books for boys of all ages' produced by the Greater Great Western in 1923 , by W. G. Chapman. This is a second edition copy, issued in September 1923, in which was added a note on the new 'Castle' class engine. *Author's collection*

Below: The publicity material of the 1920s included this jigsaw puzzle, depicting *Caerphilly Castle,* produced in 1924. It was sold only in the GWR kiosk at the British Empire Exhibition, price 2s 6d,

Left: During the short period of 'Castle' supremacy on the 'Limited', 1923-7, No 5005 *Manorbier Castle* heads the up train on the sea wall at Rockstone Footbridge, east of Dawlish. The first two coaches are wood- and steel-panelled 'toplights' and the third is a 'concertina', the stripes on it being the inset doors. *LPC*

Centre left: This is an early view of the down 'Limited' hauled by a 'King', possibly No 6003 *King George IV*, in the autumn of 1927. The photographer thought it was *King George V*, but she did not receive the coil springs visible on the bogie until after going to America and acquiring the famous bell. The location is Taplow station. *F. W. Curtis*

Below: The up 'Limited' on the climb from Burlescombe to Whiteball Tunnel on 26 August 1928. No 6008 *King James II* was only six months old, but it looks as if there was a crisis in preparing her for this run. On top of the firebox, a washout plug cover has been wrenched up and is hanging on by one screw. At the rear of the train is one of the 1924 seven-coach sets, and the St Ives and Falmouth coaches at the front are new, but there are also two 'concertinas'.
Real Photos/D. R. Barber

when 'bright young things' danced in the streets and all sorts of advantages from votes to vacuum cleaners were spreading down through the class strata. If there was still appalling poverty in areas such as Cornwall, opinion was that it was merely an aberration, and so long as business could be kept profitable its benefits would flow to the poor — provided, of course, that they flowed to the rich first.

The books included *Devon: The Shire of the Sea Kings*, a small handbook *The Cornish Riviera* intended for American tourists, and a booklet *The Ocean Coast*. The latter was distributed free in the summer of 1927, clearly as a counterblast to the Southern Railway's publicity for its new 'Atlantic Coast Express'. Very smartly got-up books on Abbeys, Castles and Cathedrals came out in 1924, and in 1928 appeared the famous books *Glorious Devon* and *The Cornish Riviera* by the popular countryside writer S. P. B. Mais. These were sold in huge quantities and are still numerous in bookshops today.

A received story among locomotive enthusiasts was that technical progress on the GWR ceased after 1914 but this was far from the truth. What happened was that Pole considered that engineers should provide what their managers requested rather than what they fancied doing. Expenditure was directed where it would encourage people to use the company's services. The locomotive is there solely to pull trains and, since at this stage experiment and redesign were unlikely to reduce the cost of haulage, they were not indulged in. Money was spent on improved coaches, Automatic Train Control, enlarged and improved passenger accommodation at stations, mechanised freight handling, new signalling — things which related directly to attraction for the customer and profitability for the company. The GWR was the only one of the four Groups which paid a consistent dividend to all its holders, an achievement for which the engineers should be given their share of credit.

Below: Double-heading was most unusual at the London end of the route, so 'Star' No 4047 *Princess Louise*, on this up Plymouth express passing West London Junction, is probably attached to the train as a means of bringing her up in a hurry for some other job. The train engine is No 6000 *King George V*, identified by her cabside medals. *Real Photos*

Above: One of the many photographs taken by H. Gordon Tidey at Twyford East signalbox; 'King' No 6012 *King Edward VI* at full speed with a 12-coach train, watched by the signalman, the lengthman and two small boys. The restaurant car, a 'dreadnought' as usual, is just behind the signal post. *LPC*

Below: At Iver on 5 August 1929. A crack train, the 1.30pm Paddington-Plymouth, may merit a new engine, No 6016 *King Edward V*, but it still has to make do with a 40ft bogie brake van at least 25 years old. *E. R. Wethersett*

It is also fair to say without disparaging him
that Collett was not a maverick like
Churchward. He suffered from poor health and
the tragic death of his wife in 1923. He had
been brought up in the little world of Swindon
Works; keeping it running smoothly was his
main aim and that he did superbly well. His one
notable blunder, the 'King' class, was forced on
him by the Board for wholly non-engineering
reasons.

The 'Limited' retained its premier status.
New train sets were allocated to it in 1923, 1929
and 1935. In 1923 the train leaving Paddington
contained coaches terminating at Weymouth,
Minehead, Ilfracombe, Exeter, Kingsbridge,
Plymouth, Falmouth, St Ives and Penzance.
This formation of nine portions was claimed as
a record, although Exeter and Plymouth cannot
really be counted as separate destinations, and it
was well behind the less-celebrated South
Western newspaper train with its 11 portions.

Demand continued to rise and by the end of the
decade a summer Saturday 'Limited' was
accompanied by three or occasionally four
reliefs, not in the timetable, all running a few
minutes apart. To be able to whistle up this kind
of extra capacity 'as required' could only be
done by a company that was comfortably
profitable.

In the autumn of 1927 the GWR was
roundly beaten in the nonstop game when the
London, Midland & Scottish Railway (LMSR)
began running the 'Royal Scot' over the 299
miles from Euston to Carlisle on a daily
booking. There was now less kudos to gain from
running through to and from Plymouth, so a
stop was added at Exeter in the winter schedule
from 1928, and there was less inhibition to
stopping at Newton Abbot to attach or detach
an assisting engine. The Kingsbridge coach was
detached at Exeter; a coach was no longer put
off at Plymouth, but a new one was added for
Newquay, maintaining the nine portions, with
the Westbury and Taunton slips as before. When
the Frome and Westbury cut-off lines were
opened in 1933 the Westbury slip took place as
the train was approaching Heywood Road
Junction, and a shunting engine had to come
out and draw the coaches into the station.

Above left: New coaches were built for the prestige West of England trains in 1929 but they only saw six years' use on the 'Limited' before they were superseded by another new train. This must have been one of their last workings, in the early summer of 1935. The up train emerges from Dainton Tunnel to drift down the incline. The engine, No 6007 *King William III*, would later be substantially rebuilt following damage sustained in the Shrivenham collision of 15 January 1936. *GWR*

Left: This photograph was released at the same time as the previous one to show the new 'Centenary' train which came into service on 8 July 1935. It depicts the up train on the bank of the River Teign, approaching Bishopsteignton signalbox. The formation is: brake composite, third (the St Ives portion), brake third, composite, first diner/kitchen, third diner, third, third, brake composite. The engine is No 6003 *King George IV. GWR*

Above: A summer 1935 view of the up 'Limited', behind No 6015 *King Richard III*. The formation is: brake composite, brake composite, brake third, composite, kitchen/first diner, third diner, third, third, brake third. It is running on the recently opened Westbury cut-off line; Fairwood Junction is just out of sight beyond the rear of the train. *Real Photos*

On Monday 23 November 1931 Paddington station and the down 'Limited' were used to start a 'Buy British' campaign, run by the Empire Marketing Board whose Chairman, J. H. Thomas, was a pal of Viscount Churchill, GWR Chairman. Engine No 6000 *King George V* carried a large headboard; the train carried an advertising display; there were ceremonies at Paddington, Exeter and Plymouth. The reception in Plymouth took place in heavy rain.

During the interwar period the schedule of the main train was not significantly changed. The Paddington-Plymouth time was reduced to 4hr from 26 September 1927 and to 3hr 57min in the 1933 summer season. In Cornwall it was largely limited by speed restrictions on the line. The Plymouth road was now so busy that speeding up one train would have demanded speeding up them all, and spectacular increases would only be possible with an enormous increase in the installed power, which in turn presumed massive expenditure on the way and works. A lot was done in this respect (again unappreciated by armchair enthusiasts), allowing Collett to introduce an enlarged 'Star' class engine, the 'Castle', in August 1923, and then in

27

August 1927 a 'Super Castle', better known to us as the 'King'. Following work on the Royal Albert Bridge in 1928, including replacing the main girders of the subsidiary spans and extra ties in the main spans, 'Castles' and the new 'Hall' class were permitted to work through to Cornwall, finally displacing four-coupled locomotives on the expresses. By 1935 the time to Penzance was brought down to its lowest ever, 6hr 15min. The summer 'Limited' was shown in the public timetable to make no stop between Paddington and Truro (279 miles) on weekdays or St Erth (299 miles) on Saturdays, but that was pure fiction as it always had to stop at Plymouth to change engines.

In 1935 it was relaunched as an equivalent of the Pullman Car trains seen elsewhere. The 'Centenary' train set carried fewer passengers than ordinary stock, at a time when even the GWR had to admit that the lower classes were travelling more. To redress the balance, the relief service running at 10.35am from Paddington and 10.10am from Penzance was made a daily fixture and given the 'Cornishman' title. It was not the same as the original 'Cornishman', which faded out before the war. This matter was further confused when, in the 1950s, British Railways used the name again for a completely different service from Wolverhampton.

The erosion of its record-holding statistics did nothing to dull the gloss of GWR publicity or the glamorous image of its foremost service. During the mid-1930s a popular encyclopaedia *Railway Wonders of the World*, sold in magazine form, included as its frontispiece a coloured diagram of a 'King', and its 17 other coloured plates included *King George V* and the 'Limited'. Pundits in the 'racing pages' of enthusiast magazines declared it to be the toughest express locomotive assignment in the country and even occasionally mentioned the efforts of that minion, the fireman, who actually generated the power that made it possible. In 1934 the GWR book *Cheltenham Flyer* called it 'the aristocrat of trains' — a telling phrase, reflecting a change in emphasis to luxury.

In 1936 Chapman brought out a book, *By Cornish Riviera Limited*, which was not issued by the company but by a general publisher, Routledge. It was at pains to take the reader 'behind the scenes' and describe railway operation to the layman, but also a defensive note had now appeared. The railways were aware that they were losing in the adulation stakes to the motor car and the aeroplane, and reiterated that speed was not everything; safety, comfort and reliability were their strengths. They resented the colossal road-building programme of the 1930s and the threat it posed to their finances. Paddington drew up plans to electrify the line to Penzance, but they knew that outlay and return would not equalise.

When war broke out someone must have done some string-pulling in high places, for of all the British train services the 'Limited' alone kept its title in the literature and on the coaches. It was, however, slowed by some 2hr 40min, rerouted via Bristol and advertised as combining the function of the 'Torbay Express' from 25 September 1939. On 16 October there was an equally drastic change back to the Westbury route, acceleration to 5hr Plymouth and 7hr 40min Penzance, and a nonstop run to and from Exeter — which once again made it the world record holder. The composition was seven coaches for Penzance and five for Kingswear, but this was soon inadequate, which was embarrassing as the track layout at Paddington made it very difficult to handle trains longer than 16 coaches. The only thing to do was to divide the train, although the 'Torbay' was not officially reinstated until October 1941. Another concession was that from mid-1942 the company was allowed to continue painting the 'Riviera' and Special Saloon coaches in full livery, while other repainting was in a dull brown. This special treatment was of course due to the numbers of high-ranking Naval personnel commuting between London and Dartmouth and

Right: The company photographer's impression of passengers dining in the Centenary train, obviously with everything including the mannequins polished to perfection. The proprieties have not been forgotten: the lady being squired so gallantly is wearing an engagement ring. The plates, glassware, cutlery and silverware all bear the GWR emblem. The table-lamp shows the intention to imitate the Pullman style but the decor, while luxurious, shows a 1930s angularity. *GWR*

Left: The up 'Limited' in August 1935, loaded to 12 coaches by the addition of a brake third and composite. 'Bulldog' No 3423, built in 1906 as No 3713, is assisting No 6012 *King Edward VI*, both engines are steaming well and both drivers are thrashing them on the ascent of the 1 in 42 Hemerdon Incline.
M. M. South

Below left: The 'Limited' was not always a showpiece; if you were plebeian enough to consider travelling on a Sunday, you had to put up with some very ordinary coaches, including at the front a Dean 'clerestory'. The engine, No 6015 *King Richard III*, is immaculate. This is the down train in Sonning Cutting.
Real Photos

Devonport — even when there's a war on, officers and gentlemen have standards to keep.

In May 1946 came a speed-up, to 4½hr to Plymouth and 6hr 55min to Penzance, which was good going considering the difficulties under which the railwaymen were working. Coal was in such short supply that it was an achievement to move anything at all. The 'Limited' was suspended altogether from 20 March 1947 and resumed on 16 June. But if the government kept the railways short of every necessity, when it finally put an end to the farce of the Groups' imaginary independence and abolished them, one

thing in plentiful supply was paint. The train soon changed colour and, for the first time, was given a headboard for the front of the engine.

The postwar train conveyed a Weymouth coach, slipped at Heywood Road as in the old days, two detached or attached at Plymouth, one or two for St Ives and the rest for Penzance. The other resorts were not neglected; through coaches for them were conveyed in other trains, for there were now more services to the West Country than ever before. On summer Saturdays the St Ives portion grew until it formed the major part of the train. From 1952 the front portion of the train,

Right: By 1938 the euphoria had subsided. The railways found that the government funding they had enjoyed had been diverted to rearmament and, worse, to the road haulage business, which they regarded as decidedly unfair competition. So they launched the 'Square Deal' campaign, which was embraced by all the companies, as can be seen by the identical wording on the Southern Railway van at the cab road exit at Paddington station. There is another banner on the footbridge at the far end of the roof. This shows the fourth arch, added in 1910, a much plainer structure than the original Brunel/ Wyatt station. On the nearest column, the hoarding reads: 'Daily Telegraph — BRITISH REPLY TO GERMAN TRADE DRIVE'. This was in December 1938. *GWR*

Centre right: The oil-burning era. Only four four-cylinder 4-6-0s were converted to oil fuel during the crisis of 1947. On Monday 25 August 1947, No 5079 *Lysander* approaches the platforms of Marazion with the up train, laying the continuous smoke trail which seemed the usual product of oil firing. The heads out of the second and third coaches suggest that some passengers knew that this was a special operation. The leading coach is in wartime paintwork, but the rest are keeping the old standard and the fifth is a 'Centenary'. *Rev A. C. Cawston*

Below right: A new look. The up 'Limited' at Bishopsteignton on 28 July 1948. New coaches of the Hawksworth type with straight sides make up the formation except for the kitchen and diner. The 'King', No 6026 *King John*, is painted blue, with BRITISH RAILWAYS on the tender, and has a numberplate on the smokebox door. *P. C. Short*

10 coaches, reversed at St Erth and went down to St Ives. Two or four coaches for Penzance formed the rear portion and were detached at Truro. But although St Ives received a 'Cornish Riviera Express' in the afternoon, it did not despatch one in the morning. The 10.30am Paddington-St Ives and the 10am Penzance-Paddington were named 'Cornish Riviera Express' while the 11am Paddington-Penzance and the 9.20am St Ives-Paddington had no name.

In 1954 British Railways celebrated the centenary of Paddington and 50 years of the 'Limited'. They put a plaque on the wall beside Platform 1, next to the passenger enquiries office, unveiling it on 29 May to mark the anniversary of the completion of Brunel's station. On 1 July special headboards were put on the engines, which had been somewhat cleaned up, and a commemorative brochure was handed out. The staff at Newton Abbot depot celebrated the occasion in their own way by providing an especially dirty engine to pilot the down train.

On 8-11 March 1955 test runs took place to a 4hr Paddington-Plymouth schedule to see if that hallowed time could be restored, using No 6013 with 14 coaches to Westbury and 12 onwards to Plymouth on the down run, and 12 throughout on the up run. They did not keep time on the first try, but on the second down run on the 10th they ran through Exeter 8min ahead of time in 2hr 39min. The schedule was put into the summer timetable; the down train was genuinely nonstop, but the up was assisted from Plymouth to Newton Abbot.

This set the stage for the last performances of the original production, an era when, as seen in these pages, many railway lovers flocked to take their photographs, for they knew that in a few more years, business efficiency would wipe adventure from the stage and the show would be over.

Left: Another postwar change: a train reporting number. The down 'Limited' at East Park Farm, just after passing Twyford. It is 31 December 1948 and, austerity notwithstanding, holiday travellers swell the train to 13 coaches. The 'King' sports one of the first hand-painted examples of the British Railways lion emblem. *E. C. Ive*

Above right: In 1951, Festival of Britain year, the dirty old-fashioned steam train was nobody's favourite; look at the grimy state of No 6003 *King George IV* on what was supposed to be the premier job. The first, fourth and fifth coaches are 70ft 'toplights', with 60ft 1938 coaches between. This is the up 'Limited' at Twyford on 5 July. *B. Morrison*

Centre right: This up express, calling at Camborne in July 1950, is a mixture of periods. 1936-built No 6809 *Burghclere Grange* is followed by a 1946 Hawksworth coach and behind that a 1905 'dreadnought'. On the Wyman's bookstall is a poster: 'Radio Times LOOK before you LISTEN'. This refers to radio; television, although 20 years old, was still an upstart of low status in the BBC. *G. Clarke*

Below right: By 1952 the train had been smartened up, with headboards, clean engines and Hawksworth stock, excepting the 1938 kitchens and diners. No 6028 *King George VI* is on the down working at Langley on 5 June. *E. R. Wethersett*

THIS PLAQUE WAS UNVEILED
ON 29ᵀᴴ MAY 1954
TO COMMEMORATE THE CENTENARY OF

PADDINGTON STATION

DESIGNED AND BUILT BY
ISAMBARD KINGDOM BRUNEL
ENGINEER OF THE GREAT WESTERN RAILWAY

Top & Above: In 1954, two special headboards were made for the 'Limited' and carried on the trains on one day only, 1 July. No 6017 *King Edward IV* did the up working from Plymouth and 6018 *King Henry VI* was on the down run. The latter is seen standing on the down through line at Newton Abbot, waiting for an assisting engine to back on. Inspector Joe Cooper and the driver are standing beside the cab. *J. D. Blyth*

Left: In 1954 it was again permissible to take pride in your history (after the surge of Coronation fever the year before), so this stone was put up in Paddington station. Its unveiling was one of the events of the International Railway Congress held in London from 19-26 May. *IAL*

Above: The up 'Limited' climbing to Whiteball on 23 July 1955. In the summer everything with wheels was pressed into service, and in this 13-coach train the first four are all different types. The engine is No 6027 *King Richard I*. They had even run out of train number boards at Laira, and the number 635 is chalked on the front. On the track, the down line has been partly resleepered and has the short fishplates introduced in 1935, whereas the goods loop is getting pretty dilapidated. *K. H. Leech*

Below: The cold air of 16 March 1956 condenses the steam from No 6004 *King George III*, approaching Newbury Racecourse station with the 11-coach down 'Limited'. The cloud at ground level is coming from the exhaust steam injector, which is a sensitive device and frequently wastes a small dribble of steam. *A. E. Brown*

Above: Evening light at Dawlish in September 1955. The train is an up express from Kingswear composed of new British Railways standard coaches, with No 6025 *King Henry III*. It is emerging from Kennaway Tunnel and about to run through the station. On Marine Parade, a prewar Standard and a Ford contrast with the shape of a new Morris Oxford — the sleek modern image soon to be embraced by British Railways. *P. Ransome-Wallis*

Left: Paddington station was, as Brunel said, 'all in a cutting, admitting of no exterior'. This is the frontage in Praed Street of the Great Western Royal Hotel, through which you walked to emerge in a makeshift back yard called 'The Lawn', flanked after 1933 by two cubist office blocks. Facing you then was the open south end of the station roof. *IAL*

2. The Setting

From the urban canyon of Paddington to the seashore vistas of Penzance and St Ives was a sweeping scenic contrast, and similar extremes were seen in the style of the railway. However, most of the environs of the line were rural and the publicity made the most of it. In *Through the Window*, the book describing the scenery on the route, we are assured that 'the country has now assumed a pleasantly open character' and that was at Hayes, 11 miles from the start.

Paddington was built in the valley of the West Bourne, one of London's maltreated rivers. It was designed by I. K. Brunel, soon after he had been on the committee for the design of the Great Exhibition, and he said it was derived from Joseph Paxton's Crystal Palace, although in appearance it owes more to the pioneer iron and glass Palm House in Kew Gardens. The lack of any provision for offices and amenities was its weak point; there was no circulating area at the platform ends and with all the facilities

extending along the west (departure) side, the east (arrival) side became neglected and unsavoury. The tracks were below street level, and remained so until beyond Ealing; thus the traveller did not see the sort of townscape which was revealed in all its glory on the way out of, for example, Waterloo.

West of Ealing lay the valley of the River Brent. This was where the ceremonial first sod of the Great Western Railway was cut in

Below: Paddington had no decent buildings; all it had was the roof, inspired by Paxton's Crystal Palace. Originally, the middle arch contained sidings, linked by turntables and transverse tracks which passed through the cross arches. The original electric arc lamps, which feature in the famous painting 'The Railway Station', are still in place. Over at Platform 5 is one of the 'Milford Boat Train' sets introduced in 1900. This is a view south from the west side. *Real Photos*

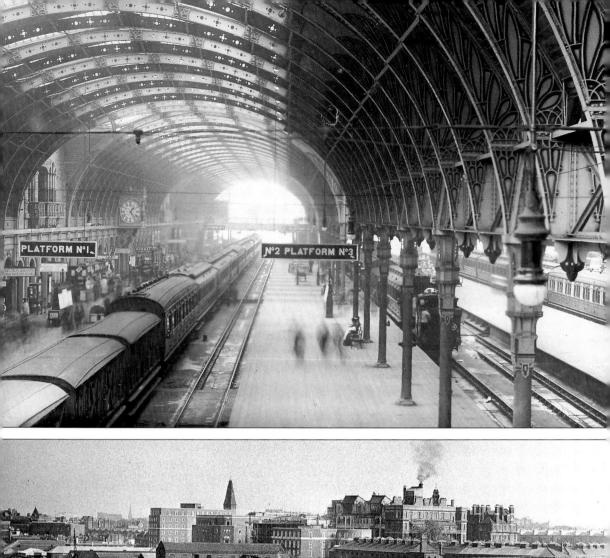

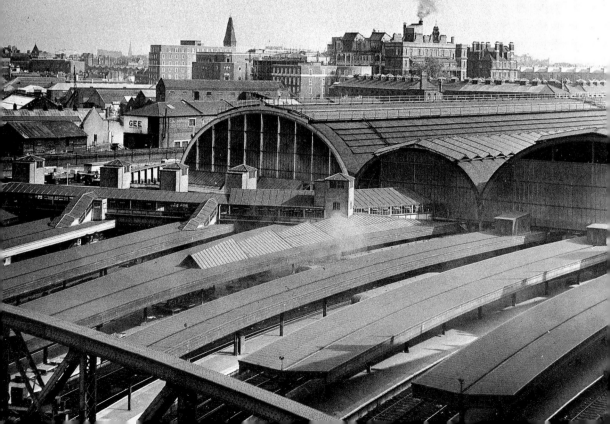

Above left: A view from the south end of the roof, taken between 1910, when the three-face clock was installed, and 1923, when the War Memorial was erected. The offices are strung along beside Platform 1. The train, the 1.30pm to the West of England, has a slip portion; the slip coach is identified by two long cylindrical vacuum reservoirs on its roof. *LPC*

Left: Successive enlargements of Paddington brought the large fourth roof arch on the east side, the platform extensions with low awnings and the diagonal footbridge leading to the Metropolitan Railway station off to the left. In the distance, to the left of the building labelled GEE, may be seen the water of the Grand Union Canal Paddington Basin. This view was taken in September 1951. Note the GWR diesel railcar in Platform 5. *M. W. Earley*

Above: No 4074 *Caldicot Castle* running into Paddington's Platform 10 in about 1930, before the signalling was replaced by colour lights. Above her is the main building of the Metropolitan Railway Bishop's Road station, and above that the huge office block of Paddington Goods. *Real Photos*

September 1835 by Lord Wharncliffe, so the viaduct over the valley was named after him. This long viaduct was needed to maintain the railway on an even gradient which over that stretch was 1 in 1,204. This almost-level was obtained until reaching Sonning Hill, between Twyford and Reading. Here a vast cutting was necessary and Brunel compromised by allowing the line to rise at 1 in 892 to a summit and fall at 1 in 792 into Reading. He could have taken the line closer to the River Thames, but he was also concerned to keep a straight alignment. He envisaged trains of up to 1,000 tons and speeds of up to 100mph, which seemed quite fantastic at the time — that was why critics condemned him as extravagant. He has since been proved right.

Another of Brunel's grandiose schemes which later generations have had reason to bless was the 'one-sided' station, in which both up and down platforms were on the same side of the line and were entirely separate. The practical inconvenience of the arrangement is obvious, but the space occupied by the layout came in useful as trains grew longer, for there was room

Above: An express pulling out of Paddington shortly after World War 2. The gantry of colour light signals was installed in the 1931 resignalling scheme. The engine, 'Star' No 4028 *King John*, was renamed *Roumanian Monarch* in 1927 but lost that name in 1940. The coach is in the postwar livery. *H. Gordon Tidey*

Below: An express on its way out of London past Wormwood Scrubs on 9 March 1930; engine No 4083 *Abbotsbury Castle*. Behind the train the exit tracks from Old Oak Common Carriage Depot rise to the flyover in the right background. Behind the wall is Kensal Green Cemetery, burial place of I. K. Brunel. *E. R. Wethersett*

Above: An up express passing through Slough station in about 1912. The engine is No 3405 *Mauritius*, rebuilt in 1902 to form the prototype of the 'City' class. *LPC*

Below: In the meadows of the Thames Valley, the 'Limited' roars past Sonning Box and on towards Reading. This is the winter 1930s formation: No 6003 *King George IV* has '14 on', of which four will be slipped before reaching Newton Abbot and the steep South Devon inclines. *Real Photos*

for enlargement. The last one-sided station was Reading, rebuilt into conventional form as late as 1895. Of the stations on this first section, Slough was given special attention because it was used by royalty for their early train journeys from and to Windsor and remained the junction for the later Windsor branch. The GWR turned snobbery into an art form. When *Through the Window* came out in 1924 it listed the stately homes beside the railway, 54 of them, and the names of the gentry owning them, with the implication that they would be friends of ours.

The 'Berks & Hants' line followed the course of the River Kennet and the Kennet & Avon Canal, through Newbury and on to Devizes. Also using this route was the Bath Road, so it was a transport corridor of ancient origin. The railway ran past rich riverside meadows, arable fields and sweet-turfed upland downs, up to a summit in Savernake Forest and on down the Vale of Pewsey. This part was not, of course, constructed as a high-speed through route and it was fortunate that the curves and gradients were easy and required little adaptation. Not that they were negligible; it was continuously uphill for 31

Above: A spot favoured by photographers was the bridge carrying the Bath Road over the Berks & Hants Line, south of Reading West station, where engines were opened up to accelerate away from the junction. The train is the 10.40am Paddington-Newquay; engine No 6010 *King Charles I*, first coach a 1923 70ft third, second coach a 'concertina', third coach a 'dreadnought' brake third. It is passing the Southcote Junction distant signal. *Real Photos*

miles westbound from Southcote and for 27 miles eastbound from Westbury, which for the engine crews of expresses demanded continuous steaming with no let-up.

When the sections of the Devizes branch from Reading to Patney, the Wilts, Somerset & Weymouth from Westbury to Castle Cary and the Yeovil branch from Durston to Langport were joined up and turned into a main line during 1903-6, the work was done to a high specification, and the completed line had no speed limit. All the same, it is interesting to note that in October 1951 the new Patney-Westbury

Above: In the heart of the Wiltshire countryside the Midland & South Western Junction Railway crosses the GWR main line. This view looks east from Wolfhall Junction signalbox along the main line, the curvature exaggerated by the telephoto lens. Curving off to the right is the connection to Grafton South Junction on the MSWJR. The train is the 10am Cheltenham Spa-Southampton on 4 July 1956, comprising a brake third, corridor third, brake composite, brake first and a '4300' class engine. *S. Rickard*

section had to be dismantled completely because its foundations were inadequate and waterlogged, something from which Brunel's original works did not suffer. Another feature of this line was that it did virtually nothing, financially speaking, for the district through which it passed. On the old route the towns, including Didcot, Swindon, Chippenham, Bath, Bristol, Weston and Bridgwater, continued to grow, but the Berks & Hants remained rural, untouched by the stream of expresses that raced by its villages.

Whether you descended from the tunnel under Somerton Hill, or crossed the miles of marshy moors from Nailsea, you came to Taunton, a crossroads town and the start of the West Country. A promontory, extending for 140 miles; that is, nearly the distance that Scotland extends north from Perth, but only a fraction of the width. As you go down it you feel, if you have a nose for these things, that you are going further and further from the mass of England, away from its crowds, its industries and (as residents down there are well aware) away from sources of fuel and raw materials. As you progress through this island within an island the air grows moister, the lanes narrower, the hills steeper, even the railway grows more winding, and the pace slower; and if there be people who do not relish it, frankly, they would do better to stay out.

The 57 miles between Cogload Junction and Aller Junction caused irritation to managers and a lot of overtime for traffic and locomotive staff every summer, for all the holiday trains from London and the Midlands coalesced on to it. A flyover was built at Cogload in 1933. Work on one at Aller began in 1914 but was cancelled;

Left: Savernake station, serving Tottenham House and the village of Burbage. The up 'Limited' passes on 4 August 1952, its engine running with steam shut off and the blower on to recover steam pressure after the long climb from the Somerset levels. The train appears to be all Hawksworth stock apart from the kitchen and diner; the engine is No 6029 *King Edward VIII*, just about the only memorial to that unhappy monarch. The down signal is a curiosity: owing to the confined space, both its arms are centre-pivoted. The tracks curving away to the right are the branch line to Marlborough. *G. W. Goslin*

Above: Taunton: a view from the long footbridge west of the station on 15 July 1957. To the left is the four-track main line, to the right carriage sidings and the engine shed in the distance. There are down trains in Platforms 1 and 3, and a pannier tank is attaching coaches to an up train in Platform 6. 'Hall' No 4978 *Westwood Hall* is propelling the empty coaches for the 6.20pm all stations to Exeter into Platform 5. *R. E. Vincent*

the separate Plymouth and Torbay lines from Newton Abbot were altered in 1925 to a main and relief layout with a flat junction, which meant that if anything went wrong on the short and overcrowded Torbay line, down trains could block back to the junction at Aller and then Plymouth trains would be stopped as well. A great deal of the 1929 Government cash was concentrated here, covering four-tracking from Cogload Junction to Norton Fitzwarren and enlargement of stations at Taunton, Cullompton, Sampford Peverell, Tiverton Junction and Exminster. In 1935 design work began on a scheme to rebuild Exeter again to nearly twice the size and to construct a new line from Exminster to Newton Abbot inland of the celebrated sea wall section. For its abandonment we can, ironically, thank the war, for if it had been built that wonderful run round the coast would have been lost to railway passengers and to walkers on the wall — a welcome change to soulless persons who love nothing but speed but a disaster to everyone else.

Of course, congestion was acute on only a few days in the year, but that was when large numbers of people elected to travel and, receiving what they perceived as an inadequate performance by the railway, were discouraged

Above: The junction at the west end of Norton Fitzwarren station on 5 September 1959. The Minehead line curves right, the Barnstaple line goes straight on and the Exeter line curves left. The 9.20am Saturday through train from St Ives to Paddington, the up equivalent of the down 'Limited', hauled by No 6008 *King James II*, is passing. There is evident congestion on the down line; the signalman has cleared his signals for a train but at Victory Crossing, the next box to the west, the signalman has not cleared his, and a train is waiting on the down relief line. *P. Poulter*

Below: Minehead terminus, situated where the railway could go no further along the coast owing to the huge bulk of Porlock Hill, rising behind the station in this view westwards. The wide platform was built in 1928 to serve holiday crowds, but of course for most of the time it looked like this. On 22 August 1961 a '4500' places a van by the loading dock. To the left can be seen the engine facilities: a water tank and, far left, a turntable. An engine shed previously stood beyond the tank. Note, on the platform, a GWR seat with the WR painted but not the G. *M. Hale*

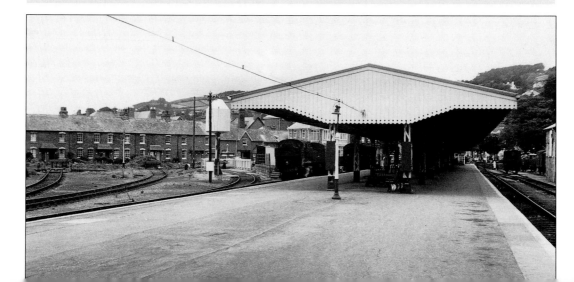

Above: A view on the under-appreciated Taunton-Barnstaple line. Although this was taken outside our period, on 22 August 1964, it shows a scene that changed little over many years. The Saturday 10.12am Ilfracombe-Wolverhampton through train, hauled by 2-6-0 No 7303, starts away from Venn Cross. It is unlikely to have done any business, as the station is four miles from the nearest village. On the right is an example of a signal arm pivoted in the centre, used in confined sites; the lamp and red/green glasses are mounted lower on the post to make them visible under the bridge on which the photographer is standing. *M. J. Fox*

from extending their use of it. On the map, extra capacity existed; the Barnstaple, Tiverton and Exe Valley branches linked Norton Fitzwarren with Stoke Canon, and the Teign Valley branch went from Exeter to Newton Abbot via Heathfield. These minor lines were never uprated and were proscribed not only for larger engines but also for 70ft coaches, so they were used only as diversions in emergencies.

Where an alternative route would really have been useful was along the South Devon sea wall.

If you want a level route for a railway, the shoreline is an obvious place to look, but with a cliff on one side and the sea on the other, it is an expensive one. Dawlish Warren, a sandbank protruding into the Exe Estuary, would not now exist at all were it not for the efforts of the South Devon Railway and GWR to protect their property. The sea breached the wall on several occasions, the first at Breeches Rock in 1846 and the last at Powderham in 1936, and track washouts were routine. The South Devon Railway had an Act of Parliament making it an offence to remove any soil, shingle or rock within 60 yards of the sea wall, or even to dig in the sand within 40 yards of it, between the Warren and Teignmouth, on pain of a £10 fine.

In view of the narrow shape of the peninsula and the maritime element of its economy — not to mention the emphasis on seaside attractions in the tourism drive — it is an oddity that once the train turned inland at Teignmouth no view of the open sea was presented to the windows until it ran through Marazion station on to the shore of Mount's Bay, or curved round the cliffs at Lelant to emerge above St Ives Bay, with the

exception of a brief sight of the briny as it passed above Par Harbour. Minehead passengers saw the sea, if the tide was in, for their last few miles, and Ilfracombe passengers, if they leaned out of the window, saw the sea ahead and below with apparently nothing to prevent the train from diving into it.

Water there was in plenty: great tidal estuaries of the Teign, Plym, Tamar, Lynher, Tiddy and Hayle, graceful rivers such as the Dart and Fowey, and countless little streams trickling down, invisible in the bottoms of the valleys they had created. Those valleys were crossed by banks, bridges and the viaducts for which this route is famed. The succession of pictures in the windows as the train came out of each cutting delighted holidaymakers, while bored businessmen reflected sourly that every time they seemed to be getting up a bit of speed the brakes would go on yet again for a corner.

When the 'Limited' began running, the line west of Exeter was still much as it had been built, with sharp curves, Brunel longitudinal-sleepered track, wooden stations and short platforms at even the main stations of Newton Abbot, Plymouth and Truro, where already longer trains were having to draw up. But it was

Above: On the west side of the Blackdown Hills, the down 'Limited' emerges from Whiteball Tunnel and races down past the refuge sidings and signalbox. On this day, 27 June 1953, the man at Old Oak Common could not find enough train number boards, so he chalked the number 130 on the front of engine No 6021 *King Richard II. J. G. Hubback*

Above right: An up Class D partially-fitted freight at Burlescombe on the climb to Whiteball from the west, on Wednesday 17 June 1959. At least 46 vans are visible behind the engine, 'Hall' No 6913 *Levens Hall*. Beyond the train are two gates marking the sites of the sidings to Westleigh Quarry, where some of the supposedly vanished broad gauge track was discovered in the 1980s. The quarry branch was originally 3ft gauge and had its own engines kept in a shed on the site of the cattle pen on the right. *J. F. Loader*

Right: Silverton in the Culm Valley had staggered platforms. This view from the bridge shows the up platform. The oval toplights in the signalbox windows and the elaborate barge-boards on the timber office building show that these are old Bristol & Exeter Railway structures. Note the once-common sign 'Public Telephone'. No 5967 *Bickmarsh Hall* passes on a down parcels. *R. C. Riley*

Left: Perhaps the most photographed secular building in Devon is the Cowley Bridge Inn. Shortly after World War 2, No 6004 *King George III* brings a down express over the junction where the South Western route to Plymouth leads off to the left. *E. Oldham*

Centre left: Exeter St David's, north end. On 23 May 1959 the fireman of No 4922 *Enville Hall*, working the Penzance-Wolverhampton 'Cornishman', pushes his coal supply forward during the stop. His engine is filthy but the first coach is a spotless BR standard brake composite. The timber-clad building on the left is a goods shed. Beyond is Exeter Middle signalbox, a wooden box on a brick pillar, and the roadway in front of that is Red Cow Crossing. Almost hidden by a line-up of lamp, water crane and signal gantry is one of the Southern's 'E1/R' engines ready for banking on the incline to Central. Beyond that is Cadbury's Distribution Depot. *M. Mensing*

Below left: Exeter St David's, south end. On Sunday 1 September 1957, an up train runs in, over the Exe Bridge, to stop in the up main platform. It is thought to be the 1.10pm from Penzance, with coaches from Kingswear in front of the brown and yellow set; engine No 5052 *Earl of Radnor*. The 1 in 37 incline to Central curves up to the left and behind the engine is Exeter West signalbox. The signal has two 'backing' arms for shunting movements out of the up platform on to the down and up lines. The tracks to the right lead to the goods lines and loco depot, a layout cramped by the proximity of the river. *J. C. Way*

A splendid prospect of Dawlish, seen from Lea Mount. The view extends right along to Langstone Rock, a piece of the cliff that was chopped off by the railway builders and now stands isolated. Beyond that is the Exe estuary with Exmouth on the far side. Dawlish station is partly hidden by steam; Coastguard and Rockstone footbridges can be seen. On Marine Parade is a selection of period cars, including Morgan, Austin Seven, Riley, Ford Anglia, Ford Prefect, Austin Cambridge, Austin Countryman and Morris Minor. The train is the 10.10am Wolverhampton-Penzance, hauled by No 7924 *Thorneycroft Hall*, due through just after 4pm, on Sunday 17 April 1960. *J. C. Beckett*

Left: A 1930s view north from Rockstone footbridge, of a secondary express; a mixture of 'dreadnought', 'toplight' and 'clerestory' stock hauled by No 4088 *Dartmouth Castle*. The cliff here was originally vertical but was cut back to this angle in 1919 — an action which precipitated the rock falls it was intended to prevent. *LPC*

Centre left: The up 'Limited' in the Centenary period, passing secluded Coryton Beach, between Coryton and Kennaway Tunnels. The curves here were treated with great respect and provided with illuminated speed-restriction signs. *LPC*

Below left: The southernmost of the five tunnels between Dawlish and Teignmouth was Parson's; at its southern end was a signalbox which was switched out for most of the year. The train is an 'Ocean Liner' special, a variegated scratch set hauled by 'County' No 1012 *County of Denbigh*. *R.W. Beaton*

Above: Teignmouth station was built in a cutting with tunnels at each end. They were opened out in 1883 to allow for the extension of the platforms, which ended up very long and sinuous to take the lengthy holiday trains. This is the Saturday 11.55pm Manchester-Plymouth, arriving on Sunday morning, some time soon after nationalisation. The engine, No 2979 *Quentin Durward*, was built in 1905 as a 4-4-2, rebuilt to 'Saint' standard in 1912 and scrapped at the end of 1950. *E. D. Bruton*

Below: Teignmouth, seen from Shaldon Bridge at about the turn of the century, with a wonderful group of sailing vessels beached or at the quays. A down express of the latest stock is hauled by No 3050 *Royal Sovereign*, one of the short-lived 'Achilles' class 4-2-2s built in 1899 and scrapped by 1915. *H. Gordon Tidey*

changing fast, the biggest job being the doubling of the single main line. The South Devon began doubling in 1860 and did Rattery to Hemerdon in 1893, but the section from Dawlish to Parson's Tunnel Box was left until last because it contained the five tunnels, Kennaway (205yd), Coryton (227yd), Phillot (49yd), Clerk's (58yd) and Parson's (513yd). Widening the tunnels began in 1903 and double line working commenced on 1 October 1906. The whole of the Cornwall and West Cornwall route was single until the mid-1890s; the short length from Devonport to Royal Albert Bridge Box was changed to double in July 1903. Work was under way between Truro and Probus and was completed by May 1904. Fifteen miles remained: Saltash to Wearde, done in February 1906; Drump Lane to Redruth, done in December 1911; Penwithers Junction to Chacewater, done in July 1914; Gwinear Road to Hayle, done in 1915; Ponsandane to Penzance, done in July 1921; St Erth to Marazion, done in June 1929; and the last piece to be doubled, Scorrier to Drump Lane, done in April 1930. From Wearde to St Germans the original line was replaced by a completely new double track section, brought into use in May 1908. Finally, trains were travelling over just 30 chains of single track; the Royal Albert Bridge. There were many minor realignments, most in conjunction with the rebuilds of Brunel's famous timber viaducts. Some of the latter survived to carry the 'Limited' or parts thereof. Forder, Wiveliscombe, Grove, Nottar and St Germans Viaducts on the section replaced by the Wearde deviation did so for four years; Penzance Viaduct lasted until 1921, and work did not start on the Falmouth branch until 1923; Penwithers, Ringwell, Pascoe and Penryn were filled in while Carnon, Perran, Ponsanooth and Collegewood — the last in 1934 — were rebuilt in concrete.

In 1904 the main stations, although much improved as lately as the 1880s, were already inadequate for the increased numbers of trains scheduled and the crowds they would, it was hoped, bring; typically only two or three through platform roads under a gloomy timber roof, pokey wooden offices and a cramped goods station. The GWR did not regard preservation of architecture as a desideratum, and with the opening of the Frome by-pass the only remaining timber roof under which the 'Limited' passed was Exeter St Thomas. Paddington was given an additional four platforms under a new roof section in 1910-16; in 1929-33 the platforms were extended round the curve past Bishop's Road to increase maximum train length to 16 coaches and two huge modern office blocks were raised. Taunton station was doubled in size in 1931. Ilfracombe and Minehead stations were enlarged in 1928. Exeter St David's was completely rebuilt in 1911-14; additions and extensions continued until 1940. Newton Abbot was reconstructed in 1925-27 to become the archetypal Great Western station with three broad, canopied platforms and a handsome three-storey stone-dressed office. Plymouth North Road was enlarged in 1908 and 1921, then given new buildings in 1928 and two additional platforms in 1939. At Penzance the railway expanded repeatedly, both by buying land and by driving back the sea. Long Rock locomotive depot was built in 1914, Ponsandane goods sidings opened in 1937 and a new station was built in 1937-38 with only the roof of the old one remaining.

Even if your train did not stop at Newton Abbot for an assisting engine to back on in front, high-speed running was at an end from this point. Through South Devon it wound its way, with lush fields on one side and the foothills of Dartmoor on the other, while passengers either

Left: During summer in the 1930s the 'Limited' was followed down by another express for Penzance at 11am. Here it has surmounted the climb of Dainton Bank, come through the short summit tunnel, and is commencing the 1 in 40 descent towards Totnes. The train engine, No 5081 *Penrice Castle*, is assisted by a 'Bulldog' attached at Newton Abbot. The other side of the large notice board reads: 'All down goods and mineral trains with 35 wagons or less must stop dead here.' *M. M. South*

Centre left: The 'Cornish Riviera Limited' on a typical summer day in 1956 or 1957; the formation is the usual one of eight BR Standard coaches, GWR kitchen and dining cars, hauled by a 'King' class engine. It is seen in the much-photographed setting of Dainton Bank, climbing the 1 in 49 gradient past Dainton distant signal. *J. Scott-Morgan collection*

Below left: From 22 April 1958 the 'Limited' was hauled between London and Plymouth by North British 2,000hp diesel-hydraulic locomotives Nos D600-D604. However, this picture shows the new Swindon-built D803 *Albion* ascending Dainton bank on a trial run in 1959. The train is loaded to 11 coaches — one more than was allowed for the 'King' class. *J. Scott-Morgan collection*

Above: Totnes, famous among tourists as a medieval town, is to enginemen a place whence, having got down into, they have to get up out of again. A freight, conveying a load of china clay from Bovey Tracey, pulls out westwards to tackle Rattery Bank. The train engine is No 4991 *Cobham Hall*. The banker, 2-6-2T No 4165, is on Newton Abbot No 2 turn, assigned to spend the morning banking from Totnes to Brent. *R. E. Toop*

Below: Brent, junction for the Kingsbridge branch and a welcome sight for the crews of the summer Saturday procession of heavy trains, for the worst of the climbing is over. On 4 August 1956, the 8.17am Carmarthen-Penzance is hauled by 'Castle' No 5071 *Spitfire*, one of the wartime renamings, assisted by No 6813 *Eastbury Grange*. (Carmarthen and Penzance are 140 miles apart but the train journey is 321 miles.) *T. E. Williams*

Above: Brent station on 31 August 1954; a view from the south side looking over the River Avon to the foothills of Dartmoor. The Kingsbridge branch train makes its 12.24pm departure: the regular 'B' set, two cattle wagons and a van hauled by 2-6-2T No 5542. On the left a ballast train, with pannier tank No 1608, has shunted into the goods shed to await a path up the main line. *J. F. Oxley*

Below: Spring in South Devon; the western approach to Brent station, the short Brent Mill Viaduct over the River Avon. On Saturday 21 April 1956, No 7904 *Fountains Hall* brings an up express in, past the end of the up refuge loop. *D. S. Fish*

Right: Brent Hill, just over 1,000 feet, lowers over the farmland in this view, looking north from the main line summit at Wrangaton. For No 6017 *King Edward IV*, on the 9.30am Paddington-Plymouth on 30 November 1956, it is downhill for the next 12 miles to Plymouth.
D. S. Fish

Centre right: On the fringe of Dartmoor below Ugborough Beacon, Bittaford Platform was an unstaffed halt serving a hamlet and a large mental hospital. The up 'Limited' passes on Thursday 7 August 1956. No 6009 *King Charles II* and No 4924 *Eydon Hall* are making plenty of smoke, obscuring the platform and the brand-new BR standard coaches. *T. E. Williams*

Below right: The appearance of the line here is deceptive, for Nos 6988 *Swithland Hall* and 6017 *King Edward IV* are slogging their way up the 1 in 42 incline out of Plymouth, passing Beechwood with Hemerdon Siding and the summit in sight. This is the up 'Limited' on Sunday 5 August 1956, with nine BR standard coaches, the two from Plymouth in front, and the 1938 series kitchen and diner.
R. J. Blenkinsop

exclaimed with delight or grumbled that it took just as long now as it did years ago. Eventually it dropped down to the River Plym, beside which lay the freight yards of Tavistock Junction and Laira, and the locomotive depot, then up through Plymouth. North Road station was lacking in grandeur; it was never given commodious new buildings like those of Taunton, Exeter or Newton Abbot, as the South Devon/Cornwall terminus of Millbay was regarded as the principal Plymouth station right up to 1939. The chord across the top of the approach to the latter, immediately west of North Road, was built in 1876 to enable LSWR trains to reach their station in Devonport, and the 'Cornishman' was one of the first GWR trains to use it. The technical revolution of the 1890-1910 period had an explosive effect on Plymouth, which doubled in size during that time.

Leaving Plymouth for the west, your train climbed out past Devonport, with a view over the Navy dockyard and the mass of shipping in the Hamoaze beyond. Although it is going outside our period, it is amusing to note that Weston Mill Viaduct here later suffered an unusual sea-change. Whereas several viaducts were removed by tipping around them, in this

Above: From Tavistock Junction, in the distance below the town of Plympton in this view, the line enters Plymouth alongside the River Plym. It here follows the route of the earlier Plymouth & Dartmoor Railway, whose course is marked by the rubbish in front of the trees on the left. At this point, Laira Junction, goods loops diverge on this side of the line; that they are goods-only tracks is shown by the rings on the signal arms. The Sunday 'Limited' passes on 5 August 1956. With only eight coaches on, there is clearly no need for 'Britannia' No 70018 *Flying Dutchman* to be assisted by No 4908 *Broome Hall*, so the latter is probably being returned to Laira Depot after a Saturday extra working. *R. J. Blenkinsop*

case the viaduct remained intact but the water beneath it was driven back, until a newcomer would not guess that it once stood over a tidal creek.

It is difficult to say anything about the Royal Albert Bridge that has not been said many times before, especially when one has to declare an interest and aver that it is the most beautiful bridge ever built. It owes its setting to there being no comparable crossing place over the River Tamar for nearly five miles upstream. Its form was evolved from Brunel's experiences on

his first major bridge, Clifton, and in helping his friend Robert Stephenson on the Britannia Bridge. We say 'evolved' because its later custodians have found that, even using modern computers, its behaviour cannot be calculated. It owes its appearance to being made of wrought iron (although the subsidiary spans were rebuilt in steel in 1928). The grey protective paint used gives it a sombre presence, often in tune with the surroundings; the fact is that the sky in the West Country is frequently cloudy and the water beneath the bridge is grey. If you want 'pretty' you will be inviting disappointment, but grace, dignity, even drama are in the scene, and to a large extent this sets the theme for the rest of Cornwall.

The hilly nature of the road began immediately out of North Road with the 1 in 59 ascent to Devonport and it was as hard one way as the other, although at least on leaving Penzance one had three miles of level in which to warm up the engine. The major summits were at the Bridge, Bolitho, Doublebois, Treverrin Tunnel, Burngullow, Grampound Road, Buckshead Tunnel, Wheal Busy and Redruth.

Although the line passed through the heart of the Camborne-Redruth mining area, by 1904 the mining boom had passed and, with a few exceptions, the roofless engine houses stood silent with grass and furze at their feet. No one regarded them as a valuable heritage; most were used for target practice by the Americans during World War 2. From the dizzy height of

Moorswater Viaduct one looked down on the Liskeard & Caradon line, hanging on although the reason for its existence had gone and it finally closed down in 1917. The burgeoning industry was china clay, first encountered at Par. From Par station, where the track was barely above sea level, the train climbed past Par Harbour with a row of clay dries by the line; close by on the other side was the highest brick structure ever built, the 235ft chimney 'Par Stack'. Possibly the railway management took a disliking to it as more trains began passing by, for in 1907 it was knocked down. Books made much of the white tips of the clay works, seen on the high ground as the train laboured up the long bank through St Austell. This contrasted with the peaceful, wooded Glynn Valley or the undulating farmland on the way down to Truro. From the open and often windswept uplands of the mining district came the long descent to Hayle, described as 'a busy port with iron foundries' in 1924, although the famous works of Harvey & Co, beneath the viaduct, was abandoned in 1909 and lay silent and unwanted. Then came the finale. The train ran down through a cutting, through Marazion station, and emerged on the shore of Mount's Bay: a howling wasteland in winter rain, but on a fine evening with St Michael's Mount in the sun at one end and St Mary's church above the grey town of Penzance against the bright sky at the other, it was the epitome of the land of romance and legend.

Left: The rear half of this train, about to enter Mutley Tunnel, is at the site of Mutley station, the original station for Plymouth until North Road was built. The train is the 2pm to Paddington, the engine is BR 'Britannia' No 70016 *Ariel* and behind her is an LMS coach. The big building on the far side of the road is the Infirmary. Note the absence of cars on this day, 27 June 1955. *R. E. Vincent*

Below left: Plymouth North Road station on 27 February 1928, showing the 1908 buildings with the platforms extended round the curve in the distance in about 1921. The arrangement faintly echoes Brunel's idea of separate up and down stations: in the gloom under each roof is a single track with platforms on both sides. The middle track is a reversing siding, leading into the down line at this end and the up line at the far end. Rising up out of the picture is the down main starter signal post, with repeater arms low down where they can be seen from close to. By the rail in the foreground are three detonator placers, used in conjunction with the signal, so that if a driver were to receive the 'right-away' from the platform staff and move off while the signal was still at danger, he would be alerted by three loud bangs. Lurking coyly under the platform on the left is Milepost 246: the distance from Paddington via Bristol. *GWR*

Right:
At Wingfield Road in the western suburbs of Plymouth, the South Western line diverges at Devonport Junction and immediately denotes its identity by the lattice-post, upper-quadrant signal. Heading down the GW line is the 4.5pm Plymouth-Saltash railmotor, two 1909 70ft auto-trailers hauled by pannier tank No 6420, on Sunday 5 August 1956. *T. E. Williams*

Below: Shunting in progress at Liskeard on 24 June 1955. 2-6-2T No 4523 has brought some wagons of china clay up from Moorswater and has now drawn a van, possibly a 'Bloater' fish van, from a short siding serving the shed where the lorry is parked. It is highly unsatisfactory to have to use the main line but the yard, which extends round to the left, is crammed in on a hillside ledge. Immediately beyond the train but invisible is the Liskeard Viaduct. The station is well equipped with directions to the Looe branch; you go along the up platform, then by a path past the water tank and round to the left. *R. E. Vincent*

Above: Derrycombe Viaduct, the sixth of the line of eight viaducts on the section between Doublebois and Bodmin Road. This view was taken on 21 April 1954, and 40 years later would be unrecognisable. The Forestry Commission are making a road up to the right in preparation for covering the whole of this side of the valley with conifers. As the gradient post shows, it is 1 in 69 steepening to 1 in 59 at this spot; No 6817 *Gwenddwr Grange* is drifting cautiously down the hill with a 22-wagon Class F freight. The first wagon is a BR pallet van with pressed steel ends, whereas the third is a GWR van. The fifth is a 'Fruit A' van and the seventh and eighth are cattle wagons. *B. A. Butt*

Left: The 11.5am Plymouth-Penzance stopping train on 14 June 1956, drawn by No 1006 *County of Cornwall* (then based at Laira depot, which was close to Cornwall if not in it), stopping at Lostwithiel — viewed from the station footbridge. The creamery on the up side was opened by Nestlé & Co in 1932. Milk tanks are berthed on the down side. Note the immaculate signalbox with its roof finials — in front of it is a station nameboard with old rail posts — and the crossing gates with cast-iron posts on the left. We do not know who the trader in the van is but he is based in St Austell. *M. Mensing*

Right: Par, the junction between the Cornwall Railway and the Cornwall Minerals Railway, later known as the Newquay branch. In this undated view a passenger train for Newquay waits in the branch platform while a long freight train works past it on to the curve leading to St Blazey Depot. The train engine is out of sight behind the goods shed and a pannier tank is assisting at the rear. The regular branch passenger set is berthed in the goods shed. In the background the main line rises on a 1 in 60 incline towards St Austell.
B. A. Butt

Centre right: A view of Truro c1950, showing the position of the cathedral above the confluence of the Rivers Kenwyn and Allen. The railway runs past the top of the town, with Carvedras Viaduct on the left and Truro Viaduct on the right. *Author's collection*

Below right: At Truro a large chunk was dug out of the hill in 1900 to produce a site for a depot. A footbridge across the site made a superb viewing platform. Left to right are the coal stage, three-road engine shed, engine repair shop, three-road wagon repair shop and marshalling yard. On this date, 15 May 1959, there are at least 11 engines of 'Grange', 'County', '4300', '4500' and '9400' classes in the yard.
M. Mensing

Left: Perranporth, in the midst of a mining area, tried to transform itself into a holiday resort in the 1920s, although it was handicapped by having only a single track line linking it to Newquay and Chacewater. This view looks north towards the two-mile-long beach. *Author's collection*

Below: One of the delights of Cornwall is the long light evening; solar time is 20min behind railway time and the sunlight reflects off the sea to give an extended twilight. The sun is still bright at 8.15pm on 16 May 1959, as the 7.15pm Newquay-Truro pulls out of Chacewater station on to Blackwater Viaduct. The engine is 2-6-2T No 5552 (now preserved at Bodmin). The corridor brake third coach No 1638 has a compartment at this end, with doors on both sides, which has been designated 'ladies only' by BR. *M. Mensing*

Right: Newquay, just after World War 2, looking across Towan beach towards the harbour. The harbour tramway came out of the cliff on the left and on to the pier. The massive block on the hilltop is the Atlantic Hotel. In the foreground the cliff has been eroded through to leave an isolated block, called 'The Island', on which a house stands, accessible only by a slender suspension bridge. *Author's collection*

Centre right: Camborne station, looking west, in July 1950; a GWR brick building on the right, a West Cornwall timber building beyond, and the goods shed obscured by the down platform awning. Pannier tank No 7422 is shunting. This type was a version of the standard shunting engine adapted for road service, with smaller cylinders, a smaller boiler but a larger, shallower firegrate. *G. Clarke*

Below right: Some parts of west Cornwall can look pretty bare and forbidding, like the setting of Gwinear Road station. In this view looking west, in June 1920, the Helston branch engine has left the coaches in the branch platform on the left and shunted two vans across to the up main. Enamel advertisements on the end of the building include Bovril, K Boots 'the best for all', *Daily Mercury*, *Evening Herald*, *West Briton* 'largest circulation', Jaeger Boots & Shoes, Henry Lawrie Ltd wholesale ironmongers of Plymouth, and Criddle & Smith of Truro and Newquay. *Real Photos*

Left: Hayle station, seen from a bridge over the cutting west of the viaduct. The derelict buildings below the viaduct on each side are the foundry of Harvey & Co, the great Cornish engine builders. The 4.15pm all stations Truro-Penzance is accelerating away. The engine, 'County' No 1023 *County of Oxford*, carries a polished diamond on her smokebox door; she was the diamond of Truro Depot. *B. A. Butt*

Above: The scene at St Erth on the morning of 19 April 1952. Passengers from St Ives have disembarked from the branch train, the B set with engine No 4566 (now preserved on the Severn Valley Railway) standing in the bay. The up 'Limited' hauled by 'Britannia' No 70019 *Lightning* is running in. St Erth is a loading point for spring broccoli, carried in cleaned out cattle wagons. In the yard is a collection of 'MEX B' wagons; the two nearest are the oldest, of a type dating from 1879, the third is an 1888 version and the fourth and seventh to ninth are of the last, 1929, design. *B. A. Butt*

Right: The St Ives branch winds through the cliffs of St Ives Bay. It comes through the notch in Carrack Gladden on the left, under the Porthrepta Road and over a viaduct behind the Carbis Bay Hotel. *Author's collection*

Left: St Ives station, showing almost the whole layout except the engine shed, whose roof is visible at bottom left. The engine release crossover is in the shadow of the station building; branch trains stop at this end of the platform and the rest of its 630ft is used only on Saturdays when the through trains come in. *LGRP*

Below: At Marazion during the period when 'Britannias' were used on the 'Limited'. No 70019 *Lightning* passes with the up train on 18 June 1952. Returnable fruit boxes are piled up in the yard. *C. M. Shoults*

Above: Penzance is famous for the Broccoli Specials, whose legendary status was consolidated by the BTF film 'Train Time'. In the yard by Ponsandane Crossing, a farmer is loading broccoli and conversing with a member of Bousfield Bros staff, whose store is on the left. In the mid-1950s, tractors — a Ferguson and a Fordson — have only recently replaced horses. The first two wagons on the right are GWR 'MEX B' cattle wagons, followed by a BR standard van, a 5-plank vacuum-fitted open, then a BR van with extra ventilators and sliding doors for loading palletised fruit. *R. C. Riley*

Right: The railway separated eastern Penzance from its seafront, with only two crossings to give access. This is Long Rock Crossing in June 1950, with No 7909 *Heveningham Hall* passing on an up express. On the right is the coal stack of Long Rock Locomotive Depot, which lies behind the train. *B. A. Butt*

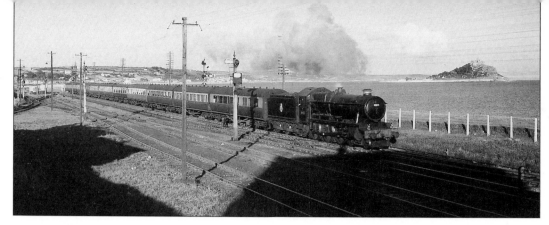

Above: The evening sun of 1 July 1950 lights the whole curve of Mount's Bay, with St Michael's Mount rising from it like a fairy-tale castle. The Mount has a village and harbour on its landward side and is linked by a causeway to Marazion, visible behind the indicator signal, centre. Coasting into Penzance is a relief to the Wolverhampton 'Cornishman' hauled by No 1004 *County of Somerset*. On the far left is the shunting neck of Long Rock Depot and at the end is a tank wagon in the Shell-Mex siding. *B. A. Butt*

Centre left: Some of the GWR engine names seem a mite whimsical, although doubtless the owner of the original *Didlington Hall* took it seriously. The up 'Limited' of 17 April 1954, at Ponsandane Crossing on the way out of Penzance; No 6940 has a full load of 14 coaches. The sea is behind the fence on the left, and Chyandour is in the background. *B. K. B. Green*

Left: Penzance station soon after World War 2, looking down towards the 1879 roofed station and the platforms, lengthened in 1937 during the holiday boom. The train leaving is the 12.20pm milk to Kensington, hauled by No 6826 *Nannerth Grange*; it has only a light load but will pick up more on the way. On the left is a passenger brake van allocated to the Paddington-Penzance TPO. *J. Davenport*

3. The Players

The first train in Britain equipped with gangways connecting between the coaches was built at Swindon in 1892. The coaches were luxurious by the standards of the day, with gas lighting, an electric bell communication from each compartment to the guard, and separate ladies' and gentlemen's lavatories. In 1893 more coaches were built for the 'Cornishman': six-coach sets and three-class composites for the Falmouth through coaches. There were no restaurant cars; those only appeared on the GWR in 1896 after the abolition of refreshment stops.

These were the coaches in use on the West of England expresses at the start of 1904. However, as soon as Dean retired, Churchward ordered radically different American-style vehicles, with no doors into the compartments but access via vestibules at each end and in the middle. It was a requirement that the door handles, etc, did not protrude beyond the loading gauge and that, should a door come open, it would remain within another, larger, envelope and not strike lineside structures. Consequently the doors were inset in the maximum width bodies. The roof shape was new, the traditional GWR clerestory being replaced by an elliptical structure. They were built to the maximum dimensions the loading gauge would allow: a body width of 9ft 6in and overall length of 70ft. They were, indeed, the largest coaches which have ever run on British railways. They were nicknamed 'dreadnoughts' because that was the name of a much publicised, very large, heavily-armoured battleship built for the Royal Navy at this time, and anything massive-looking was called a 'dreadnought' by the British public. The first examples in service were kitchen/dining cars released in May 1904. When the 'Limited' was inaugurated on 1 July it presented an incongruous aspect, with the solitary 'dreadnought' in the middle of a rake of standard coaches, looking like a well-endowed music-hall dancer in a line of prim elderly ladies. Uniform seven-coach sets began running in the summer of 1905. These carried first- and third-class passengers but no seconds, presaging the demise of second class.

The new coaches were criticised by the traffic staff, because their size severely restricted

Below: A typical GWR coach used on expresses at the time of the creation of the Cornish Riviera. No 1602 was a 56ft second/third corridor composite, built in July 1900 to Diagram C15. As built, it had four lavatories, one each end and two in the middle, the latter of which were for ladies only. This view shows the corridor side. It was taken outside the paint shop at Swindon Works; the transverse rails under it are used by the traversing table which lifts coaches across to the access sidings. *GWR*

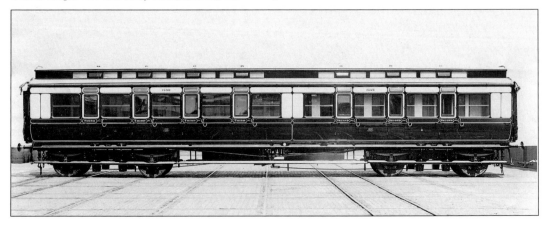

their route availability; by the lay press, who pointed out that travellers did not like mingling with a random selection of (probably vulgar) humanity when boarding and alighting, and by the British public because they were different. Churchward clearly thought that the civil engineers would be obliged to go around enlarging bridges, moving platforms, easing curves and bringing the whole railway up to the standard of the few main lines — just as he thought the British people would embrace open-plan living. It did not happen and he had to compromise. The next stock saw the return of compartments with individual doors. With a row of inset doors the coach side presented a pleated effect, so these coaches were dubbed 'concertinas'. They included slip coaches, which ran in the 'Limited' from 1906.

The 'concertina' design was obviously unsatisfactory, so a new body profile with flush doors was built from 1907. The distinctive external feature was a small hammered-glass pane above each main window, so these coaches were called 'toplights'. New sets were built for the 'Limited' in 1914, although 'dreadnought' restaurants were still in regular use in the 1940s. In later years, a 'toplight' with one-piece windows and its panelling replaced by steel sheet

Above: No 3433 *City of Bath*, the engine on the 1903 nonstop Paddington-Plymouth run. She was built in March 1903 and scrapped in September 1928. *IAL*

Above right: 'Atbara' class No 3381 *Maine*, built in May 1900 and scrapped in September 1927, is seen during the first two years when she had the interim Churchward boiler with a square firebox and a parallel barrel. The tender is older than the engine and has two stanchions for the old emergency passenger communication cord. They are now used for a piece of wire to help restrain the coal stack. (Coal space on tenders is never adequate.) *LPC*

cladding was very little different from a BR standard coach designed 50 years later.

A similar revolution took place in locomotive design. The GWR four-coupled bogie express locomotive of 1899 differed little from Robert Stephenson's 1830 'Planet' design, but in that year two new 4-4-0 locomotives, 'Badminton' class No 3310 *Waterford* and 'Bulldog' No 3352 *Camel*, were fitted with a new type of boiler comprising a square firebox, a barrel with no steam collector dome and a cylindrical smokebox. This was the fruit of researches by Churchward's assistants G. Pearson and

J. Cross. Before long it was revised with a barrel tapering from rear to front; this type was first used on 2-6-0 No 2662 in 1902 and thereafter fitted to most new locomotives and to many older ones when replacement boilers were needed. From 1910 the boilers incorporated superheaters.

For the mechanical part of the engine Churchward was also planning something new, derived directly from American practice. It was much larger, with an extra pair of coupled wheels. These wheels were mounted in conventional frames, but forward of them were two big castings, each incorporating a cylinder, valve chest and half a curved saddle to support the front of the boiler. The castings were symmetrical, a pair joined back to back. To their front were attached short American-style bar frames to carry the leading bogie and front bufferbeam.

The first of these engines, No 100 *William Dean*, completed in February 1902, had outside cylinders but inside valves and motion, and as built had a parallel boiler. The second, No 98, completed in March 1903 (later named, appropriately, *Vanguard*), carried a taper boiler and had much larger valves with a travel twice that of any previous British locomotive. The

valve chests were moved outside the frames but the motion was still inside, and this remained the pattern for all subsequent large Great Western locomotives. A third, No 171 *Albion*, appeared in December 1903 and a production batch was built in 1905.

Not all the GWR Board shared Churchward's American obsession. Widely regarded as the best locomotives in Europe at the time were the compounds being built by the Société Alsacienne des Constructions Mécaniques of Belfort in France, to the designs of Alfred De Glehn. The Chairman, Earl Cawdor, bought three of these of the 4-4-2 or 'Atlantic' type. The first, No 102 *La France*, was shipped over in October 1903 and entered service on 2 February 1904. Inasmuch as De Glehn was English born, the locomotive was more English than Nos 100 and 98, and certainly looked it. On test she ran at 85mph on the level and attained 50mph up Whiteball Bank. Churchward was impressed by her performance but concluded that it derived not so much from the compound system as from the high boiler pressure and the mechanical layout; a view confirmed by two more examples bought in 1905 which, although larger, did not perform any better. Whether in a genuine spirit of

Left: An 'Atbara' with the improved type of boiler in which the firebox tapers from front to rear, the barrel tapers from rear to front and feed-water clacks are mounted on the top adjoining the safety valves. This design of boiler was fitted to new engines until 1956. No 3377 *Kitchener*, built in May 1900 and scrapped in April 1930, is seen at Tilehurst in March 1926, then numbered 4124, hauling a heavy train of milk vans and 'Syphons'. *M. W. Earley*

Below left: No 1201 was a 70ft Ocean Liner luggage van, built in October 1910 to Diagram M15. It was later used for mails from Plymouth and finally for newspapers. This view was taken after World War 2, as the chalked 'OOC 8-44' on the frame testifies. *IAL*

enquiry, or from a wish to show that the home team could do just as well, he had Swindon build a similar sized four-cylinder simple engine, using standard parts where possible. This was No 40 *North Star*.

The configuration was that of the De Glehn compounds, with two inside cylinders mounted right forward to drive the leading coupled axle and, to make the connecting rods the same length, outside cylinders attached just where the frame was cut away to clear the leading bogie. To be strong enough to take the piston forces, this assembly needed a massive bracing structure inside the frame plates, through which the valve motion was threaded. The result was a nightmare of inaccessibility which haunted fitters responsible for examining and repairing the 'Limited' engines for the next fifty-odd years.

To make closer comparison with the French 4-4-2, No 40 was built in April 1906 as a 4-6-0, but could run as a 4-4-2 with the rear axle removed and replaced by smaller trailing wheels, carried in a sub-frame bolted to the main frame. Some of the two-cylinder engines were also so fitted. This seems rather whimsical in hindsight, but it was within the memories of those involved

Above: Swindon publicity photograph of the French Atlantic No 102 *La France*, as assembled in late 1903 and painted in photographic livery before being put to use. *GWR*

when even four-coupled wheels were not thought necessary or even practical for fast running. Experience proved the six-coupled arrangement superior, so it was as a 4-6-0 that the design went forward. The two-cylinder type was termed the 'Saint' class and, with its successors the 'Hall', 'Grange' and 'Manor' classes, totalled 445 engines; 274 four-cylinder engines of the 'Star', 'Castle' and 'King' classes were built.

Nos 100, 98 and 171 worked the Paddington-Plymouth leg of the 'Limited' until the spring of 1907, when new 'Stars' came out of the shops and took over this top-rank job and stayed on it until 1923. The Plymouth-Truro and Truro-Penzance legs were worked by Churchward-boilered 4-4-0s of the 'Bulldog' class. The Cornish lines were unable to accept longer or heavier engines, a situation which persisted until the 1920s.

Another engine design associated with the 'Limited' was developed during this revolutionary period. No 95 was a 2-6-2 tank engine, built in 1905, using the same paired cylinder block structure and taper boiler. She was followed by a batch of 20, Nos 2161-2180, which were the last locomotives built by Wolverhampton Works in 1907-8. These engines were later known as the '4500' class and for the next 50 years were part of the West Country scene. They were small enough to go almost anywhere and were lively performers. They worked all kinds of traffic on both branch and main lines in Devon and Cornwall, and hauled the 'Limited' through coaches on the Kingsbridge and St Ives branches. In the mid-1950s a pair of '45s' hauled the 10 coaches of the Saturday down 'Limited' into St Ives. In spite of the presence of this foremost express on the St Ives branch, the company did not think it merited any improvement and to the end even the similar but slightly heavier engines numbered 4575 onwards were barred from it.

By 1904 Churchward had got to thinking he could change anything for the fun of it, so *La France* was painted in an all-black livery with which he proposed to replace the time-honoured green. He did not win that one, but he did manage to monkey around with the coach colours. I. K. Brunel was supposed to have chosen the brown colour himself and the ivory upper panels were added by Gooch in 1864. The brown was replaced by a chocolate lake in 1903, then the ivory was discontinued in 1908, then they changed to a crimson lake in 1912.

One of Felix Pole's first orders was to restore chocolate and ivory and repainting began after winter overhauls. By April 1922 a 'Limited' comprising 10 70ft 'toplights' headed by a 'Star' with lining and brass decorations refitted really looked the part, albeit slightly marred by 'concertina' slip coaches at the back.

Above left: The French Atlantics were later given Swindon boilers. The boiler had to be mounted high off the frame, hence the crude expedient of putting the whistles at an angle to keep them within limits. From 1907 until scrapping in 1927 these engines were employed on Oxford expresses. This is No 103 *President*, bought in 1905, being pulled out of Paddington on the rear of the empty coaches after arrival. *IAL*

Above: A 69ft 'dreadnought' corridor third. No 3277 was built in August 1905 and scrapped about 1950. This was one of the general service batch, equipped with gas lighting for which cylinders are visible under the frame. The corridor is on this side in the left-hand half and crosses to the other side in the other half. A legend above the right-hand bogie reads, 'not to run between Birmingham & Stourbridge or below Landore.' *British Railways*

New 70ft coaches were put on at the beginning of 1924. They were run in seven-coach sets comprising a brake third, third, composite, restaurant, composite, third, brake third. Some of these were notable as the only GWR coaches to have automatic couplers. A feature of the body design was that the end was curved outwards to bring the centre section, with the corridor connection, closer to the adjoining coach, so vehicles of this era are given the term 'bow-ended'.

On commencement of the 1929 summer season the 'Limited' was completely re-equipped, including the slip coaches. The new stock looked very up-to-date, with smooth body panelling, recessed chromium-plated door handles and the fussy 'toplights' replaced by big picture windows. Length was reduced to 60ft but, built to maximum width, the coaches were still severely restricted as to permitted routes. The formation was: brake third, third, third, third diner, kitchen, composite diner, composite, brake third (Penzance), brake composite (St Ives), brake composite (Falmouth), brake composite (Plymouth), slip composite, brake composite (Weymouth).

The kitchen had a full-length coach all to itself. The fashion at the time was to regard a train as not so much a conveyance with catering but more a mobile restaurant. This was in response to the growing competition from road coaches and cars in long-distance travel.

From 1912 the Cornwall main line accepted '4300' class 2-6-0 engines, which worked the principal expresses. When prewar standards were resumed in 1921, some 'Saints' and 'Stars' were placed in Cornwall for a few weeks, and on 3 October the up 'Limited' was taken from Truro to Plymouth by No 2937 *Clevedon Court* while the down train was hauled by No 4022 *King William*.

With business looking up after the postwar slump there was a use for a more powerful engine; with changes in top management and the restructuring of the railway it would be a good time to impress the public with another blast of statistics. Swindon produced a larger boiler for the 'Star' and bored out the cylinders by an inch and a half. These items could be fitted retrospectively and were used in new construction from mid-1923. The first new engine was No 4073 *Caerphilly Castle*, a name carefully chosen to butter up shareholders of South Wales railway companies who had been forced to join the inferior English concern. Since the larger boiler might be expected to consume more coal and water, a new standard tender carrying 4,000gal of water was introduced at the same time. That the fireman might be expected to shovel more coal passed without comment.

GWR publicity claimed the 'Castle' as the most powerful passenger engine in Britain on the quite false premise of the nominal tractive effort, so when in 1926 the Southern Railway 'Lord Nelson' returned a higher figure, the Board instructed Collett to give them a higher one still. The result was the 'King'.

Above: This could be the 'Limited' but it has only five coaches, all 'dreadnoughts'. The engine is No 172 *Quicksilver*, built in February 1905, in her initial form as a 4-4-2 with a saturated boiler. She was rebuilt as a 4-6-0 with a superheater boiler in 1912 and scrapped in March 1935. *Bucknall Collection*

The tractive effort was brought up to 40,300lb on paper by specifying a cylinder diameter of 16¼in. In fact the cylinder liners used did not exceed 16in, which brought the figure to 39,200, but journalists were not to know that cylinder diameters changed by a good half inch and wheel diameters by over 0an inch during the life of an engine. They put on it the biggest boiler to which the Engineers would agree. The axle load had risen from 18 tons 12cwt ('Star') through 19 tons 14cwt ('Castle') to 22 tons 10cwt; these engines were said to weigh 89 tons, but with frame repairs and extra gadgets added they later weighed up to 93 tons. The result was that they were restricted to running on the main and relief lines and prohibited from sidings and loops except those authorised, dead slow with the crew on tiptoes.

The big cylinders were certainly useful for lifting trains up the South Devon banks. The

Right: Some of the 'dreadnoughts' had exceptionally long lives and eventually wore BR livery. This is one of the first, kitchen/diner No 571, later No 9511, built in January 1905, rebuilt with steel panelling, new windows and six-wheel bogies in 1940, seen in Cardiff General station on 17 June 1957. She was scrapped in 1959 after 54 years' service. *D. M. Rouse*

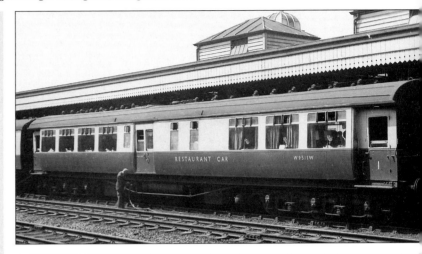

Centre right: The first GWR four-cylinder engine, No 40 *North Star*, built in April 1906 and then fitted, like the two-cylinder engines, with a temporary rear axle assembly until the 4-4-2 or 4-6-0 question was decided. She was converted to 4-6-0 and given a 'Star' boiler in 1909, rebuilt to 'Castle' standard in 1929 and scrapped in May 1957. This view shows her when new, beside the great coal stage/water tank at Old Oak Common, also new. *LPC*

Below right: No 4010 *Western Star*, the first 'Star' to be built with a superheated boiler. She was built in May 1907 and scrapped in November 1934. She is standing in the engine servicing yard at Ranelagh Bridge, outside Paddington. The driver is holding a standard GWR oil feeder. In the background is the single platform Royal Oak, which served the Hammersmith & City Line. *IAL*

81

story is that one day during the war a 'King' took 17 coaches up from Plymouth unassisted, and on another day No 6011 *King James I* got a packed 17-coach 'Torbay Express' grossing 650 tons over Whiteball Summit at 25mph.

No 6000 *King George V* worked the 'Limited' down to Plymouth on Wednesday 20 July 1927, taking 10 coaches through nonstop as a demonstration, but was then packed off to show the flag in America. Five more engines were already available, having been laid down at the same time. 'Kings' were rostered on the Paddington-Plymouth 'Limited' from then until 18 June 1958.

In 1928 Swindon resumed building two-cylinder 4-6-0s, 'Saints' with the coupled wheel diameter reduced to 6ft. This version, the 'Hall', was a better hill-climber than the 'Castle', and was well suited to handling the expresses in Cornwall. However, for prestige reasons a 'Castle' was booked for the 'Limited' when there was a good one available.

The next 4-6-0 type, the 'Grange', with 5ft 8in wheels and improved cylinders, was better still, but was not normally used on the 'Limited', perhaps merely because the job was already being done satisfactorily.

Above: A 70ft 'toplight', showing the small hammered-glass panes above the windows which give the type its name. Kitchen/third diner No 9556 was built in July 1913, rebuilt in 1936, refitted internally in 1947 and scrapped in 1958. This coach was unusual in having six-wheel bogies from new — it weighed 42 tons. *GWR*

Throughout all this time the remaining 4-4-0s were still being turned out for assisting between Newton Abbot and Plymouth, presenting a publicity malapropism when coupled in front of a gleaming 'Centenary' formation. In 1948 replacements arrived in the form of eight 'Manor' class 4-6-0s. These engines were poor performers on the banks, having a new design of boiler which was a reluctant steamer; crews took a dim view of an assistant which rapidly ceased to provide much assistance. The 'Manors' were taken back to Swindon and modified, after which they continued on the piloting job until the end of the 1959 season.

By 1955 the Western Region could no longer ignore the fact that the 'Kings' were racking themselves to pieces and it was a losing battle to keep them going. Swindon resorted to drastic action: broadly, they chopped the front of the engine off and replaced it with new frame pieces

Above: What was then described as the 'super-locomotive': No 6000 *King George V*, built in July 1927 and eventually preserved. Photographed at Swindon on 1 August 1927, before the trip to Cardiff and thence to America. Preparations for the excursion included a Westinghouse pump and an amazing amount of polished bare steel. *LPC*

Below: No 6000 *King George V* posed for the publicity photographer at Old Oak Common Depot in 1929. Most of the 1927 'bull', such as the polished wheel bosses, is still present and the paintwork includes lining-out on brake hangars and framing. *LPC*

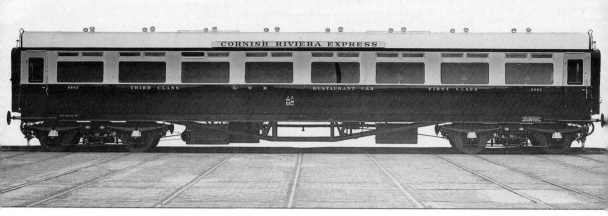

and inside cylinder castings. The plan was to rebuild 20 engines and scrap the rest; eventually they did all 30, an expensive measure for which the owners, the British public, received very little return.

Returning to 1935, the next change of coaching stock was part of the jollifications to mark the centenary of work starting on the Great Western Railway. The 'Centenary' stock was intended to be the most luxurious in service in Britain, to match the standards set by Pullman coaches, which the GWR did not use because it never bought or hired from outside what it could make for itself. Since prior reservation was required for all seats, there was in effect a fare supplement like that on Pullmans. The bodies were 61ft long and extended to the extreme permitted width of 9ft 7in. Only 25 vehicles were built; two 10-coach sets normally ran the 'Limited' in the formation: brake third, third, third, third diner, kitchen/first diner, composite, brake third, third, brake composite, brake composite.

The 'Centenary' stock continued to run during the war, until the destruction of Plymouth in the spring of 1941 shocked the railway into making formal plans for diversions of main line trains by using the branch lines.

Above left: 61ft 'bow-end' composite dining car No 9582, built in July 1929 and scrapped in about 1959. These coaches had a modern version of the old toplight but the main windows had new flush mountings. On the left of the frame is marked, '63-6X9-7 32T 17C' and on the right, 'Not to run over the eastern and western valleys not to work north of Wolverhampton or Hereford.' *GWR*

Centre left: The most luxurious coaches on the 'Limited', or any other GWR service, the Centenary stock. As a safety measure owing to the extreme 9ft 7in width of the body on these and the 1929 stock, the doors were inset and also angled in towards the end. This is third No 4582, built in July 1935 and scrapped in 1962 after spending only six years on top-rank services. *Real Photos*

Below left: Typifying the last generation of GWR stock, Hawksworth corridor third No 2273, built in April 1950, seen as running in BR red and cream livery. All these coaches were removed at the end of 1967. *Real Photos*

The maximum-width stock would have made this difficult or impossible, so, notwithstanding the need to provide members of the Admiralty with respectable amenities, the special coaches were all taken out of service. After the war they were not restored to their former position but, like their contemporaries the LNER 'Streamliner' coaches, were dispersed to work out their time in obscurity. The postwar socialist government was careful to banish these reminders of the bad old days of prewar privilege.

On Collett's retirement in 1941 the post of Chief Mechanical Engineer was taken by his deputy and former Works Manager, Frederick Hawksworth, who had not only spent his entire career in Swindon Works but had been born in the town. Swindon was proud of its continuity, but this began to look a bit like in-breeding.

New locomotives and coaching stock were promised in 1945 — but then, new everything was promised in 1945. It was August 1946 before the first Hawksworth coach appeared and deliveries were leisurely, even though Swindon, The Birmingham Railway Carriage & Wagon Co, Gloucester Railway Carriage Co and Metropolitan Cammell were building them. When the 'Limited' was next allocated a dedicated set of coaches it was drawn from the 60ft stock of 1938. The restaurant cars at this time were two of the 70-footers built in 1923. This set was painted in a garish travesty of GW livery, termed 'plum and spilt milk', as a trial by the Railway Executive. Asked for its opinion, the British public came out strongly in favour of the GWR colours. The RE took no notice.

The new engine turned out to be a pretty direct descendant of No 98, except that the Churchward cylinder block was replaced by a conventional full-length plate frame with cylinders bolted to it. Yet another coupled wheel diameter was chosen, 6ft 3in, just for a change. The boiler was similar in dimensions to the Crewe-designed boiler of the LMS 2-8-0 freight engine, with the high working pressure of 280psi to push up the theoretical tractive effort — old habits persist. The new class, the 'County' was announced as being for the Cornwall line; 30 were built and some were indeed used in Cornwall. Reading the accounts, one may see that they were either good and strong or

pedestrian and disappointing. Their most significant feature was out of sight of the enthusiasts, a hopper-bottomed ashpan.

For the summer 1956 timetable the 'Limited' was one of a selection of named expresses provided with new BR standard coaches, painted in a brown and yellow livery which adumbrated the original GWR chocolate and ivory. One set was tripped down, empty, on Wednesday 6 June so that both up and down trains began in the new colours on the 11th. That year also saw another dynamometer car run on the normal service, down on 30 May and up the following day; they were testing engine No 6002 *King William IV* with a double chimney.

The last word should go, as it did in the operation, to the tank engines which brought the empty train into Paddington station before its two-day round trip and took it out again afterwards. They all had side tanks or saddle tanks until 1910, when Swindon introduced the pannier tank. It was cheap to make and allowed access beneath it to the motion of the engine, which the conventional side tank did not. In 1904 the Paddington empty stock duties were done by a collection of broadly similar engines termed the '1901' and '2021' classes, some of them built at Wolverhampton in the 1870s. In June 1927 the Kensal Green flyover for the

Above: Such is the wilful perversity of the British public that, while the standardisation in locomotive design was dismissed as unadventurous, the progress in coach design was derided when it produced sights like this. An 1890s Dean 'clerestory' with a pronounced sag in its body is coupled to a new 1929 'bow-end', behind No 6013 *King Henry VIII*, built in May 1928. If an old coach was added to a set it was usually on the front as that was the least popular position, due partly to a fear of the first coach in safety-obsessed travellers and partly to the vulgarity of being near the noisy, smelly, dirty engine. *Real Photos*

engine and carriage lines was completed. Because of its steep gradient the empty stock workings were taken over by some 16 '4500' class 2-6-2Ts for about two years. In 1929 more powerful pannier tanks, the '5700' class, were introduced. Orders for new engines (backed by Government money) were now outstripping Swindon's capacity, so the first 50 were built by the North British Locomotive Co and the next 25 by Kerr Stuart. In 1954 they were joined by some of the new tapered-boiler pannier tanks, the '9400' and '1500' classes, built for the South Wales coal traffic. These were the last generation of steam locomotives to haul the '10.30 Limited'.

Above: In December 1924 'Saint' No 2925 *Saint Martin*, built in September 1907, was fitted with 6ft diameter coupled wheels to see if that would improve performance at low and medium speeds. This is the engine, running as No 4900, assisting No 6004 *King George III* on the climb from Totnes to Dainton on 7 August 1956. The train is the 12 noon Penzance-Manchester; the first vehicle is an apparatus-fitted mail van. Historically the most important British 20th century steam locomotive, *Saint Martin* was scrapped in April 1959 before preservation became practical. *T. E. Williams*

Below: In 1938 came a bogie-fitted version of the '4300' class 2-6-0: the 'Manor'. The design was unsatisfactory, however, and with the war intervening it was not rectified until the BR era. The 20 which were built were used on such lowly duties as banking, and in that role they appeared on the 'Limited'. On 16 June 1948 No 7814 *Fringford Manor* has assisted the down train over the Devon banks and is descending to Plymouth. The 'King' behind has just been painted in the new blue livery. *W. J. Alcock*

Above: In 1939 *King George V*, still in excellent external condition with the bright-work in evidence, if not quite so sparkling as 10 years ago, finds herself on a Penzance express including representatives of every type of coach brought out since 1905. It is on the Frome cut-off, between the B3098 bridge and the footpath to Rodden Church. *LGRP*

Below: New and overhauled engines were transferred from Swindon Works across to the running shed for testing. Here on 24 September 1955 is No 6000 *King George V* after a general overhaul. A modified smokebox with a slimmer chimney has been fitted. Other recent changes include a speedometer, mechanical lubricators and bigger exhaust steam pipes. *G. Wheeler*

Right: An amazing sight on 10 October 1953. The train is indeed the 'Limited', as proved by the headboard on No 6024 *King Edward I*, built in June 1930 and now preserved. The first coach is a 'dreadnought', built in 1905 and, 48 years young, still on the premier express. The location is the curve below Langstone Rock. *M. E. Ware*

Below: While the 'Kings' reigned on the London-Plymouth line, the Penzance portion was worked by smaller 4-6-0s west of Plymouth. No 5058 *Earl of Clancarty* was the best 'Castle' in Cornwall, so she was kept immaculately clean and whenever possible rostered on the 'Limited'. On 6 November 1950 she is drifting down past Saveock Farm towards Tomperrow Crossing. On the far left is Baldhu signalbox. *B. A. Butt*

Left: In 1945 the Hawksworth 'Counties' appeared, pretty traditional except that for no discernible reason yet another wheel diameter, 6ft 3in, was introduced. Steaming was considered indifferent but they were strong engines on the banks and did well where sustained fast running was not needed. No 1010 *County of Caernarvon* is in this milieu on 7 August 1956, lifting a return Goodrington Sands-Plymouth excursion up Dainton Bank. *B. A. Butt*

Below: In 1951 BR Standard 'Britannias' were used on the 'Limited's' Cornish section. This is No 70021 *Morning Star*, named after one of two engines built by Robert Stephenson & Co in 1836 for export to Russia but bought by the GWR, pulling out of St Erth station on the last lap to Penzance in the afternoon of 19 April 1952. The fireman has resolutely followed the custom of hanging his hosepipe over the side, even though he had to thread it through the window to do so. *B. A. Butt*

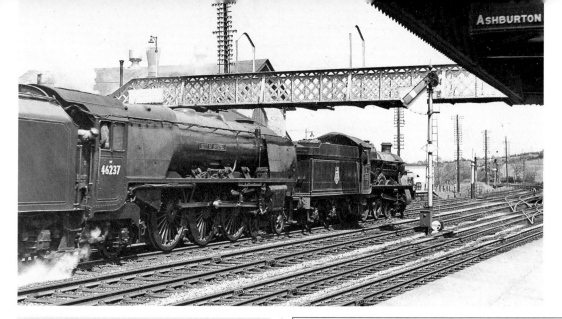

Above: Another 4-6-2 to work on the 'Limited' was the LMS 'Coronation' No 46237 *City of Bristol*. In April and May 1955 she was tested on the Bristol and Wolverhampton routes and did two round trips to Plymouth. The WR crews were keen to see what the engine could do. On 18 May they are passing Totnes at 50mph before coping with a permanent way slowing on the steep pitch of Dainton Bank. The driver of No 5915 *Trentham Hall* is relaxed, but the fireman on the 'City' is regarding with suspicion the antics of his exhaust steam injector. The cables slung along the engine are connections to a dynamometer car which was recording the run. *D. S. Fish*

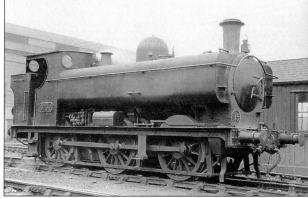

Centre right: In any review of motive power for the 'Cornish Riviera', pride of place should go to the six-wheeled tank engines, hundreds of them, ever on the move wherever there was anything to be moved. No 5764 was an early example of the '5700' class, built in 1929, and spent all her commercial life in London. She was based at Old Oak Common, where she is seen carrying one of the numbered discs which identified the engines working empty stock to and from Paddington. She became London Transport No L95 and was the last steam locomotive operated by the state railway system, when she was sold for preservation to the Severn Valley Railway on 7 June 1971. *LPC*

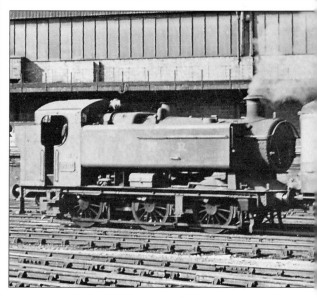

Below right: A rare view of a '9400' class pannier tank in GWR colours, which only the first 10 of the class, built in 1947, wore for a short time. No 9407 is taking an empty train out of Paddington, with steam shut off at this moment because the exit from the platforms is downhill. *T. A. Greaves*

4. The Action

Every morning the patrons of the 'Limited' arrived in Paddington station, to be welcomed by attentive porters and ushered aboard an immaculate string of coaches, whose presence they took for granted as much as they did the work of any other servants. However, while railway employees were expected to shift for themselves, coaches cost money and needed looking after, as indeed did engines. In 1904 the GWR in London was overcrowded. Paddington had only eight platform lines; as soon as a train came in it had to be whisked away to make room for the next one.

Because the through coaches in the expresses were detached from the rear on the way down and attached to the rear on the way up, when they returned to London they were in the wrong order, so the 'Limited' and many other trains had to be remarshalled every time they arrived. The locomotive depot at Westbourne Park, a mile down the line, was overcrowded and hemmed in by urban development. The carriage depots at Barlby Road and West London Junction were in the same condition. The only possible solution was to buy a big piece of open ground as near London as possible, which

Above left: At Paddington just before World War 2. A pannier tank (number tantalisingly obscured but it could be 8763) has brought in the stock for an outgoing train, has followed it down to the platform end and is now waiting for the points to be reset to take it into the pilots' siding. In the background a train is either arriving or being taken out empty. *Author's collection*

Left: The down 'Limited' settling into its stride. At Taplow, 22 miles out, the driver will have his controls set where he likes them and the fireman will be swinging his shovel regularly. The engine is No 6026 *King John* (the only 'King' not to have a number in the name) in early BR livery. The unusually elaborate shunting signal on the right is arranged so that a driver in the yard beyond can see it. *R. F. Dearden*

turned out to be on Wormwood Scrubs, three miles out. Here there grew up Old Oak Common, three-quarters of a mile long and eventually spanning some 115 tracks at its boundary facing Old Oak Common Lane. Work began in 1898, the carriage shed opened in 1905 and the engine shed in 1906, and lines of men continued to chew away the common until the spring of 1940, when the site was filled by a carriage repair works. Here were carried on not only servicing but also an endless round of shunting. Here, too, many of the hundreds of coaches which went out only on summer Saturdays, quietly passed most of their lives.

All the literature describes a sunlit smiling countryside through which trainloads of equally smiling travellers cruise without check or care; in real life they encountered darkness, rain, snow and fog — the London pea-souper lived up to its nickname every winter in the first half of the 20th century. The GWR's ability to get the trains through was in large measure due to its signalling equipment. In this, too, there was a surge of development in the 1890-1910 period. Some 2,200 signalboxes were built and equipped by Reading Works, which also housed a genius, chargehand Amos Brooker, inventor of Automatic Train Control. That went into production in 1906, and any GW enthusiast will tell you how superior it was to any other system and how disgraceful it was that 50 years later British Railways had still not adopted it; but it should be remembered that it was then installed only from Paddington to Reading. It did not reach Plymouth until 1931 and Penzance in 1939.

To placate the passengers when the scenery was less than alluring, up till World War 1 the 'Limited' had women dining car staff to tend to the ladies. In 1926 the Burndept Radio Co experimented with broadcast radio receivers on the train but this idea of 'in-transit entertainment' was not pursued.

The restaurant service was important on the 'Limited'. The GWR was late in taking up train

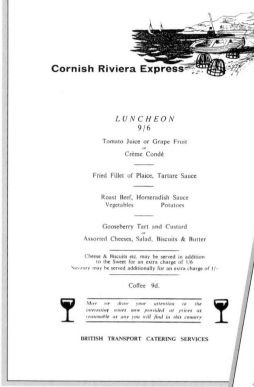

Cornish Riviera Express

LUNCHEON
9/6

Tomato Juice or Grape Fruit
or
Crème Condé

Fried Fillet of Plaice, Tartare Sauce

Roast Beef, Horseradish Sauce
Vegetables   Potatoes

Gooseberry Tart and Custard
or
Assorted Cheeses, Salad, Biscuits & Butter

Cheese & Biscuits etc. may be served in addition
to the Sweet for an extra charge of 1/6
Savoury may be served additionally for an extra charge of 1/-

Coffee 9d.

*May we draw your attention to the
interesting wines now provided at prices as
reasonable as any you will find in this country*

BRITISH TRANSPORT CATERING SERVICES

A 'Cornish Riviera' menu. Although this example dates from 1959, the elegance that characterised the heyday of the service was still there and the artwork of the brochure still echoed the style of the 1930s. Note the GWR Special Whisky on the list. *Reproduced by courtesy of I. Canavan*

WINES

When you are ordering luncheon on this train, may we draw your attention to the interesting wines offered at prices as reasonable as any you will find in this country.

SHERRY			
Medium Dry			
Amontillado No. 4, Pale Dry			
Fino No. 7, Pale Dry	Glass 2/6		
Walnut Brown	2/6		
	2/6		
APÉRITIFS	2/6		
Gin and Lime, Orange or Lemon			
Gin and Bitters			
Gin and Vermouth,			
French or Italian	2/6		
Vermouth, French or Italian	2/3		
Tomato Juice Cocktail	2/9		
Pineapple Juice Cocktail	1/9		
	Baby Bottle 1/-		
BORDEAUX Red	1/-		

	Bott.	*½ Bott.*	*¼ Bott.*
Médoc	13/-	7/-	3/9
Château Cantenac-Brown 1953			
BORDEAUX White	17/6	9/-	—
Graves			
Sauternes	12/-	6/8	3/6
	15/-	8/-	—
BURGUNDY Red			
Mâcon	13/-	7/-	3/9
Beaune	17/6	9/-	—
BURGUNDY			
Vin Rosé	13/-	7/-	—
CHAMPAGNE			
G. H. Mumm, Cordon Rouge 1952			
G. H. Mumm N.V.	47/6	24/6	—
St. Marceaux N.V.	37/6	19/6	8/6
ALSATIAN			
Sylvaner	16/-	8/6	—
SPANISH			
Spanish Graves	10/6	5/6	3/-
Spanish Burgundy	10/6	5/6	3/-
SOUTH AFRICAN			
Paarl Amber Hock			
AUSTRALIAN			
Emu Burgundy	10/6	5/6	3/-
PORT			
Tawny			
Very Fine Old	*Glass* 2/6		
	3/-		

LIQUEURS		
Van der Hum		
Cointreau		
Bénédictine	*Miniature* 4/9
Drambuie	4/3
Bolskümmel	3/9
Cherry Heering	3/9
SPIRITS	3/6
Cognac Vieux Maison, 30 years old	3/-
Brandy ★ ★ ★	
Gin	
Rum	*Measure* 3/-
Whisky—G.W.R. Special	3/-
Whisky—Proprietary Brands	2/3
Whisky—Proprietary Brands	2/3
Brandy	2/6
Gin	2/6
Rum	*Miniature* 5/-
	5/-
	4/6
	4/6

CORDIALS AND FRUIT JUICES		
Lime Juice		
Lemon Squash		
Orange Squash	*Glass* 7d.
Grape Fruit Squash	7d.
Apple Juice	7d.
	7d.

BEER, STOUT AND LAGER		
Bass, Worthington	*Split* 7d.
Double Diamond	
Other Proprietary Brands	*Bottle* 1/6
Guinness	1/6
Mackeson's Stout	1/6
Whitbread's Pale Ale	1/6
Other Light Ales	1/6
British Lager	1/3
Tuborg Lager	1/3
Carlsberg Lager	1/6

CIDER	
Cider	*Bottle* 1/8
Champagne Cider	1/8

MINERALS		
Schweppes' Aerated Water	*Bottle* 10d.
Apollinaris	*Reputed Pint* 3/6
Vichy Célestins	*Baby* 6d.
Ginger Beer	*Split* 8d.
	6d.
	9d.
	Bottle 9d.

CIGARS · CIGARETTES · CHOCOLATES

catering but, once it started, it tackled it in the grand manner. A table setting, with spotless linen, silver, china and glass, every item bearing a GW emblem, was as elegant as would be found in any dining room. Dining-car staff were an exclusive group with a corporate spirit equal to anything found in the locomotive department; cooking and serving up to 250 meals in one session is a skilled job at any time, supremely so when done in the confined space of a railway carriage, having to brace oneself all the time on a moving floor. At the end of a long, rough day a fireman could pile a heap of coal on his fire, sit down with his face dirty and express his view of the company in some choice epithets, but the chef and waiters had to be as smart, precise and attentive as they were when they came on duty. Anyone who has been involved in train operation has nothing but praise for their verve and professionalism.

The passengers the railway wanted would expect good wines with their meal. In 1906 the GWR went to whisky blenders MacDonald Greenlees of Glasgow and had an 'own brand' supply bottled for them. Under the title 'GWR Special' it was, as the menu illustrated shows, still on sale on trains as late as 1959.

From time to time, in any human organisation, things can go wrong. Sociologists may like to muse on the change evident in the fact that from the 1950s the press sought out and reported on as many breakdowns as it could find, whereas before World War 2 the railway journals and company publications simply did not mention such things but printed only the good news. They did not even remark on the work of the staff in overcoming the depredations of the elements on the railway, to which the GWR was vulnerable in such places as the Devon sea wall. Of course, the traveller, far from

applauding their efforts on his behalf, would be more likely to blame the company for allowing nature on to its premises in the first place. It was therefore necessary to minimise the evidence of even routine maintenance on the line, but sometimes the 'Limited', or more often the Sunday train, had to be diverted.

From Paddington to Reading, with two tracks available each way, it was usually possible to keep one open. Through trains by the direct route to Taunton could be rerouted via Bristol, or vice versa. Use was also made of the cross of lines between Patney, Thingley, Bathampton and Westbury, but that was inconvenient as 'Kings' were not permitted on it, so they had to find extra 'Castles' for the job. If Taunton-Exeter was closed, the alternative was via Yeovil, in co-operation with the South Western. If the South Devon line was under repair, or under water, they again had to go cap in hand to the South Western. Despite the intense competition which was the public front of the companies, they always worked together on the ground. However, while the latter was happy to accept the trains, trackside clearances and the weight restriction on Meldon Viaduct meant that almost until the end of steam working, it could take no larger GW engines than the '4300' class. On 11 November 1956 there was a blockage at Bishopsteignton; expresses were sent up the South Western and 'Castles' were used for the first time, No 4087 *Cardigan Castle* taking the 'Limited'. It seems the engineers were doubtful, for during a routine Sunday possession on

Above: With the modest-sized tenders used by the GWR, replenishment from water troughs was an essential part of the nonstop Plymouth run, and indeed of any run of significant length. This much retouched view shows a 'Saint' picking up water on Goring troughs in 1928. *Real Photos*

Left: Aldermaston water troughs, seen on 30 April 1958. The train is a push-pull, or railmotor as it was then called on the WR. 0-4-2T No 1444 propels a trailer, converted from a steam railcar or railmotor, on the 1.21pm Reading-Newbury service. These combinations were capable of running at express speeds, 75mph being quite usual, but this one is not in a hurry as it will be at Newbury half an hour before the next train, the 1.30pm Paddington-Penzance, appears. *IAL*

Right: Now it can be told! This photograph was published in the author's *From the Footplate: Devonian* to show the view from a 'Hall'. It was not on the 'Devonian' however, but on the 'Limited' on 3 May 1957. The assigned engine, No 6012, gave up at Reading and this was No 4960 *Pyle Hall*, the Reading station pilot. Kenneth Leech, who was riding on the footplate, described her as 'in a shocking state' but the driver agreed to take her and thrashed her all the way to Plymouth, frightening the inspector when he got up to 78mph. This view was taken as they struggled up to Whiteball Tunnel. *K. Leech*

Below: It happened, even on the Great Western, that on busy days engines broke down, or that they simply ran out of serviceable passenger engines to fill the rosters. On Saturday 1 August 1959, freight 2-8-0 No 3802 drifts down Dainton Bank with the 12.42pm Newquay-Cardiff express. The booked assisting engine was not needed and they could well have achieved the scheduled average of 39mph from Plymouth to Exeter. This engine has survived to be preserved on the Bodmin & Wenford Railway. *G. England*

9 December the 'Limited' was booked for '4300' haulage via Okehampton.

The plain truth is that at the best a steam locomotive cannot be expected to run for more than a few hours without attention of some sort and provision for failures was essential. As the top train, the 'Limited' had first call on any engine that was prepared at any depot; that engine's duty would have to be covered by another one, and so on. At principal stations an engine was placed on standby in the station and used for shunting while waiting for the call. During April 1936 No 2937 *Clevedon Court*, which had hauled the 'Limited' in Cornwall in 1921, took it from Reading to Plymouth on two occasions. Westbury Depot, although having no booked express passenger workings, had to keep an express engine in steam, coaled and oiled, ready to move out at 15 minutes' notice. If, however, the engine expired with not far to go, the crew would just take the nearest engine they could find; for example, on 8 October 1951 the train was taken from Hemerdon down to Plymouth by 2-6-2T No 3187 and on 12 October 1955 from Slough into Paddington by No 6113.

Above: Undoubtedly an engine failure led to this appearance of 'Star' No 4017 *Knight of Liége* struggling up Dainton Bank with eight coaches, the maximum permitted for the class, on the down 'Limited'. Steam is leaking from the piston rod glands, one of the inside cylinder drain cocks, the two inside valve front guides, and from the whistles — signs of a run-down engine. The date is given only as the year 1948. *P. L. Melvill*

One way to improve reliability was to allow the engine crew time to check round bearings, poke the fire and generally cosset their engine midway through a turn of duty. This was resorted to in the 1920s and again in the 1950s, when at both Newton Abbot and Truro the engine was replaced and took another train forward a few minutes later.

Slip-coach working was a feature of the 'Limited' throughout its career and has been described in detail in numerous publications. It was straightforward enough: the guard pulled a lever which allowed the drawhook to hinge down and release the coupling. The vacuum and steam heat pipes were sealed by interpolating a

Above: 'Kings' were allowed to take 360 tons, 10 coaches, up to Dainton unassisted. On 21 September 1946 No 6022 *King Edward III* is near the top with the down 'Limited'. At the back of the train the Dainton distant signal (by which another photographer is standing) is on, and the fireman has leaned from his doorway to look out ahead. *B. A. Butt*

gadget which when pulled split in halves, each half having a sprung valve which snapped shut. The lighting control cable was not connected. But, although the system had an unimpeachable safety record, it was still a fundamental violation of the principle of allowing only one train in a block section at one time. Moreover, it was of course a one-way process. The coaches slipped off the down train did not return on the up train, but found their way back to Paddington in a plethora of other trains. Weymouth, Minehead, Ilfracombe and Kingsbridge passengers were not granted a commensurate service up to London. Now you may feel, like this reviewer, that London is a thing to be

approached reluctantly and left as quickly as possible; but to be sensible, travel quality must be assessed both ways and is only as good as its worst part. One can only conclude that the slip system really served to allow the advertisers to quote impressive journey times from London to the resorts, and to benefit the nonstop gimmick by reducing the load of the train before it reached the South Devon banks.

Travel in the slip coach was not much of a privilege. You had no access to the dining car; the only benefit was speed, and that lasted only until the main train had cast you off. The Weymouth coach was attached to an all-stations train from Westbury. The Kingsbridge coach had a further two stages: behind a local train to Brent, where it was transferred to the branch train and reached Kingsbridge when the main train was somewhere down near Truro. The Ilfracombe coach, dropped at Taunton just before one o'clock, was attached to the 1.10pm to Barnstaple for a 1¾hr, 44-mile run across north Devon. At Barnstaple Loop Junction it was detached, not slipped this time, and shunted round to Barnstaple Junction station, followed

Above left: Most heavy trains were assisted over Dainton Bank. This example on 19 September 1953 has 10 coaches and is hauled by Nos 7813 *Freshford Manor* and 6855 *Saighton Grange*. (The limit for the 'Grange' was 288 tons.) Both have boiler pressure up to the maximum and are working very hard, and have some leakage from their glands — although it does not take much steam to make a big cloud in damp weather. Dainton signalbox is on the left; the refuge siding on the right is level and the main line comes up a 1 in 37 gradient. *C. F. H. Oldham*

Left: On 1 August 1953 a nine-coach train is assisted from Newton Abbot to Totnes by 2-6-2T No 5150; the crew have clearly put a big fire in and opened her full out to pull away from Aller Junction. The points at this end of the refuge loop are worked by electric motors, powered by a hand-cranked generator (popularly termed a 'hurdy-gurdy') in the signalbox. Of particular note on the right is a field full of traditional corn stooks. The Kingswear branch crosses in front of the field, in line with the refuge loop starter signal, and beyond it is a bus on the Kingswear road. *R. E. Toop*

Above: A potent combination of No 1006 *County of Cornwall* and No 4091 *Dudley Castle* at Dainton with the Saturday 8.20am Penzance-Paddington on 4 August 1956. The signal on the right is the down starter, placed so that drivers can see it from the sharp left-hand curve behind the camera. The track has recently been repacked and the concrete boxes between the tracks are stands for a surveyor's theodolite, to aid the permanent way engineers in keeping the level exactly right — important on a steeply graded piece of line. *T. E. Williams*

Left: A slip coach, as used on the down 'Limited'. This is the end attached to the main train. Special features are: a hinged drawhook retained by a sliding bolt; a gong, worked by the guard, to give warning of its silent approach; lookout windows, and an extra vacuum pipe, for use when working as an ordinary coach. The emergency valve, actuated by the communication chain, only works on the latter. The coach is one of the 15 'concertina' tri-composite slips built in 1906. The photograph is dated 12 April 1927.
British Railways

by another wait before it finished its journey, at about 4pm, on the back of the 'Atlantic Coast Express', which had left Waterloo half an hour later than the 'Limited' had left Paddington.

The Royal Albert Bridge had a profound effect on operations because the engine from London was not allowed to cross it. Every time the civil engineers braced it up to carry heavier engines, the locomotive engineers produced a heavier engine still, so the barrier remained. The engine was usually changed at Plymouth, although if double-heading was required through Cornwall the pair might work through between Truro and Newton Abbot. It would have saved a lot of bother if the effort put into creating and maintaining the 'Kings' had been devoted to providing engines with adequate power

combined with good route availability; however, an engine change would still have been necessary, as any engine after running 226 miles needed a break to replenish coal, water and oil, clean the fire and remove the ash.

When crossing the bridge trains carried a single line staff. When the 'Limited' started running, this and the other single sections still in use had the Webb-Thompson electric train staff. In 1914 the bridge was re-equipped with the electric key token, designed and made at Reading Works.

It was most unusual to see two engines heading a train to or from Paddington. This was partly because Great Western trains were not generally expected to run especially fast and partly owing to the magnificently level gradients

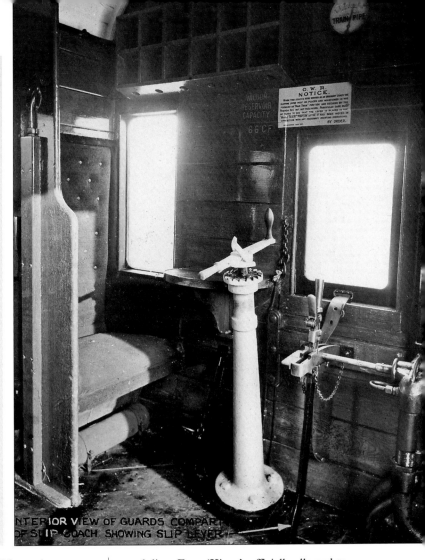

Right: A slip coach interior. The guard has an ordinary handbrake and the slip lever, which withdraws the slip bolt and controls the vacuum brake. He also has a seat where he can watch for signals, with a steam heater under it. At the top is a train pipe vacuum gauge, showing BR's 21in setting (the GWR used 25in).
British Railways

INTERIOR VIEW OF GUARDS COMPART
OF SLIP COACH SHOWING SLIP LEVER

laid out by Brunel. The critical factor in deciding whether an engine is adequate for a train is whether it can start it at any point on the route. The design of the valve motion on GWR engines gave the longest possible cut-off at full gear, making the full force of the steam available when getting away from rest, and they gave no anxiety when starting.

West of Newton Abbot the situation was completely different. A train might have to restart on a section of seven chains at 1 in 36, with sections of 1 in 49 each side of it, between Aller and Dainton; 1 in 47 between Totnes and Tigley; 1 in 42 between Plympton and Hemerdon and 1 in 37 shading to 1 in 40 for a quarter of a mile between Totnes and Dainton. These inclines were exceptionally severe for a

trunk line. Even 'Kings', officially allowed to take 500 tons from Paddington to Taunton, 485 tons from Taunton to Whiteball and 500 tons from Whiteball to Newton Abbot, were allowed only 360 tons from Newton Abbot to Brent. Therefore, assisting engines were nearly always called for on summertime loads. The GWR had what other people tended to regard as a rather fussy approach to operating practice and did not approve of pushing passenger trains from behind. On all scheduled workings the assisting engine was attached to the front of the train and was if possible a passenger engine with a leading bogie. They were provided by Newton Abbot depot, which also provided '3100' class 2-6-2Ts for banking freight trains as required and passenger trains in emergencies. Any smaller

engine than a '3100' or '5100' was not allowed to be placed on the front or rear of a passenger train, but must be attached behind the train engine.

The Cornwall main line had long stretches as steep as 1 in 60 but train loads were less and high average speeds were certainly not expected at any time. Double-heading was only resorted to if the train was well over the limit for one engine. When a train was double-headed right down to Penzance, it stopped at Marazion station or Long Rock signalbox, the leading engine was uncoupled and moved off to the depot, and the other engine drew the train into the station. This was to avoid having the back of the train fouling the points off the end of the platform. The same manoeuvre was adopted at St Ives when the main portion of the train was taken there in the 1950s, as the 10 coaches only just fitted in the platform.

After arrival at Penzance, the train had to be berthed somewhere. Even after the 1938 expansion there were only two sidings at the station and two loop lines extending down past Ponsandane yard. When they were full, coaches had to be put in the goods sidings. On peak days trains had to be taken empty to and from the sidings at Marazion, St Erth and Gwinear Road. None of these places had any covered accommodation, so staff had to do the cleaning, examining and emergency repairs in the open. Despite the growth in demand for

Right: After the slip coach has detached, the coupling and hoses on the other coach are left dangling, so extra chains are fitted to tether them. A shield is fitted over the gangway connector; the injunction 'DO NOT DROP' at the top is aimed at shunters. If you were standing on a buffer stock in the wind and rain, removing it prior to coupling coaches together, you too would drop it. *British Railways*

travel in the 1950s, no more facilities were provided and on summer Saturdays the performance at St Ives was absolutely ludicrous. The 10-coach express curved its way along the 25mph branch line, was shoehorned into the little station, then the passengers had just 10 minutes to disembark and any outgoing passengers to board, before it went back as an ordinary branch service to St Erth. It was then tripped empty to Penzance to form the Sunday 10am up. The stock off the Friday 11am down was tripped empty to St Ives on Saturday morning to form the 9.20am up.

For all the detail changes by which the management strove to assure us that everything was as up-to-date as possible, the actual running of the job did not change over the years. Lines of labourers washed down coaches while others walked through them changing antimacassars and towels. Dozens more hands shovelled interminable tons of abrasive coal and hot sulphurous ash. Drivers jammed themselves as far forward as possible in the cab to get out of the draught, leaned sideways over the reverser screw to see out of the front window and pulled over the regulator handle with the left hand. Firemen tied their trouser legs with string, stood out on the footplate open to the wind and rain and shovelled coal from a dusty heap to a hot hole; and stewards whisked the roast beef on to four plates at once or poured coffee in the swaying dining car without spilling a drop.

Above: One of the responsibilities of a slip guard in his train-within-a-train is his special double tail lamp. This one, red (left) and white (right), shows that there is one slip portion behind the main train. When it has detached, an ordinary tail lamp is shown. It was vitally important for the signalmen to see that the slips were present when they should be and that they had detached in the right places. *S. W. Baker*

Above: It has been seen before, but no account of the 'Limited' is complete without Henry Casserley's classic picture of a slip taking place. He is on the Weymouth coach which has detached on the approach to Heywood Road Junction. The main train, drawing ahead, shows a red above white tail lamp, indicating that it has two more slip portions which will detach at Taunton and Exeter. In the distance it is just possible to discern a pannier tank standing on the up line, waiting to collect the slip coach and take it into Westbury station.
H. C. Casserley

Right: On one of the single line routes travelled by detached portions of the 'Limited', Taunton to Minehead. A view from the cab of a 'Manor' class, No 7820 *Dinmore Manor*, in the preservation era. *S.H. Austin*

Left: Engines were nearly always changed at Plymouth. On 27 June 1955 No 6008 *King James II* of Laira Depot is ready for a run to London, with a generous heap of coal on the tender. From facing west on the shed, she has run from the east end round the triangle to the south of the depot and will back round the west curve to North Road station. *R. E. Vincent*

Above: The view through the cab window of a Great Western engine. No 7820 *Dinmore Manor* waits for the road, while the guard confers with the station master, and the permanent way lengthman passes on his rounds. Only the clothing of the latter gives away the fact that this is a modern reconstruction, taken on the preserved West Somerset Railway on 11 March 1999. *S. H. Austin*

Above: At the west end of the Royal Albert Bridge, at the platform end of Saltash station, is a setting-down post for the single line tablet. As this train comes slowly off the bridge, the fireman will be ready to hook the tablet on the post, while his driver keeps an eye on the suspicious character standing on the up platform end. The external finish of No 6821 *Leaton Grange* is no credit to her owners. *D. Sellman*

Left: Neglected engines burning execrable coal were not invented by British Railways, just legitimised by them. In this view in August 1949, the up 'Limited' reaches the summit of a 1 in 67 incline at Grampound Road. The fireman on the train engine, No 5055 *Earl of Eldon*, has been panicked into firing on the last stage of a climb. The assisting engine is No 7813 *Freshford Manor. P. Ransome-Wallis*

Right: A few minutes later the relief, 10.5am from Penzance, comes up the bank. No 6801 *Aylburton Grange* is managing well without assistance. The formation includes at least one 'dreadnought'.
P. Ransome-Wallis

Below: Postwar summer Saturdays brought the amazing spectacle of a full-length express on a country branch line, when the 'Limited' ran through to St Ives. On 2 August 1958 2-6-2Ts Nos 4540 and 4566 haul the 10 coaches from the main line on to the branch at St Erth. The train is made up entirely of BR standard coaches. *P. Q. Treloar*

Above: After arrival at Penzance trains had to be stabled and, since there was not much room near the station, on a summer day they would have to go up to Marazion, St Erth or even further away. On 11 May 1959, No 1005 *County of Devon* approaches Long Rock signalbox on an empty stock trip. Behind her is the water tank/coal stage of Long Rock Depot, with the engine shed to its right. The long building at the back of the train is Ponsandane goods shed. *M. Mensing*

Left: One thing you might not expect to see is one of the massive '7200' class 2-8-2Ts, more associated with coal haulage. However, No 7220 spent a while in the West Country after World War 2 and doubtless proved useful for shifting heavy rakes of coaches at holiday times. She is entering Marazion station on an empty stock trip in July 1950. The first coach is a 'toplight' brake composite, then at least 40 years old. *B. A. Butt*

Above: In some ways the 1950s saw the 'Limited' and its railway at their best, when travellers to the west reached their highest numbers ever. This is typical of the train at that time: a set of BR standard coaches in brown and yellow livery hauled by No 6025 *King Henry III*, carrying the headboard and the reporting number 130. On 23 July 1955 it drifts down from Whiteball to Burlescombe. The regulator is almost shut and traces of steam are escaping from the snifting valves, and the fireman is having a little difficulty in starting the exhaust steam injector. *K. H. Leech*

Below right: To close, a tribute to the signalmen — those patient, dedicated men who sent the trains safely on their way and without whom the system could not have worked. This view is from the window of Reading Main Line West signalbox, the largest on the Great Western Railway. The signals on the gantry are, left to right: up platform/Main Line East distant, up main/Main Line East distant, down main to down relief, down main/West Junction distant, down main to loco depot, down main to branch/Oxford Road distant, bay platforms/call-on arm/route indicator. The train, a Newbury Races special hauled by No 5001 *Llandovery Castle*, has a clear road to the branch, ie the Berks & Hants line. Appropriately, the two wagons belong to the S&T Department: a wartime 'MACAW B' bolster and, nearer, a 1914 two-plank open for carrying items such as signals. It is evident which points are provided with locks, as they have covers to protect the locking bolts from falling ash. In the up line by the engine is an automatic train control contact ramp. *C. J. Blay*

Epilogue

If you have memories of travel or work on the railway 50 years ago, I hope these pages have offered pleasant reminiscence. If the steam-hauled train is to you just a curiosity in 'history', these views may help to bring it to life and give a hint of how it was done. If you are a student, there may be some pointers for further study on and off the railway. Those in the West Country tourism industry might even find that views from the past can teach them something. If you are of the growing number of people who work with steam trains in the present, enjoy the glow of shared tradition and take this as a reminder of what you have to live up to in future.

Some of the views in this book appeared in the publisher's books and magazines when they were taken, when of course they were not regarded as 'of the past' but as contemporary. I have tried to respect them as such and not to adopt the (usually misplaced) condescension of hindsight — especially as this album is intended not to say, 'Look how we have advanced since then', but rather to say, 'This is a great achievement which happens to lie in our past.' What we need now is a time machine to enable us to go back and photograph all those details of operation of the 'Limited' which no one thought to record when they were all in a day's work!

Meanwhile, the Cornish Riviera, 'a panorama of picturesque villages, rocky recesses, golden sands, green slopes and tree-covered hills' (1904), with its 'enchanting little fishing villages, guarded by gigantic cliffs, and the long, wooded estuaries of the rivers' (1954), awaits you.

Below: Journey's end. 'Castle' class No 5058 *Earl of Clancarty* at Penzance after bringing in the down 'Limited' on 10 September 1952. *Leslie Overend Ltd*